# MATTHE

# BATTLE
# SCARS

## A Soldier's Strategy for Fighting Cancer

*JCP*

*Battle Scars: A Soldier's Strategy for Fighting Cancer* by Matthew Carr

First published in 2011 by Jane Curry Publishing
(Wentworth Concepts Pty Ltd)
PO Box 780 Edgecliff NSW 2021
www.janecurrypublishing.com.au

National Library of Australia Cataloguing-in-Publication Entry
Author: Carr, Matthew.
Title: Battle Scars : a soldier's strategy for fighting cancer/Matthew Carr.
Edition: 1st ed.
ISBN: 9780980812909 (pbk.)

Subjects: Carr, Matthew.
Australia. Army–Biography.
Soldiers–Australia–Biography.
Military assistance, Australian–Afghanistan–Biography.
Military assistance, Australian–Iraq–Biography.
Testis–Cancer–Patients–Biography.

Dewey Number: 355.0092

Cover photograph: Matthew Carr
Design: Deborah Parry Graphics
Printed in Australia by McPhersons

PEFC™
PEFC/21-31-16

## ACKNOWLEDGEMENTS

To the Troops - The nurses, scientists and well-wishers who through the years have always been at the front line, fighting this enemy alongside the battlers.

To the Captains – My family and closest friends. Leaders in your own right; you rallied my morale and stood by me through dark nights and brightly lit hospital rooms.

To my Special Forces – The surgeons and specialists whose precision scalpels and chemical concoctions have continued to hit the mark and keep the enemy well from the gates.

And most of all,
To my No 1. – Michelle my wife, for knowing me as a simple soldier and the battle that consumes me, but who loves me nonetheless.

# CONTENTS

# Foreword for Battle Scars by Matthew Carr

Every day at Cancer Council, people affected by cancer share their very personal stories with us.

Every tale is different, a testament to an individual's strength or fragility, their fear or confusion, their anxiety or their calm, their sorrow or renewal.

Matthew Carr's experience with testicular cancer encapsulates these – and so many other – emotions. His story crystallises not only the whirlwind of feelings people have at the time of a cancer diagnosis, but also their changing outlook at every stage of cancer and beyond.

But *Battle Scars* is not just about the emotional impact of cancer. It's a compelling account of a young man's adaptation to a life-changing experience – both physically and mentally. It's about the realisation that although life is fragile, there is potential strength in us all to face adversity and fight for all it's worth.

It's common for cancer to be alluded to as a battle, but Matthew has the distinction of being someone who is actually trained to go into war. His descriptions of life in the army and his deployment overseas are both a real and symbolic backdrop for his personal battles.

This story is an exploration of attitudes, abilities and adventures. Matthew's often candid and sometimes humorous explanations of cancer and survival, employment, relationships, personal growth and spirituality, are a valuable addition to the growing catalogue of cancer memoirs. These memoirs provide readers with valuable insights beyond what is possible to include in cancer information resources, such as those published by Cancer Council NSW.

I commend *Battle Scars*, not only for its ability to touch on so many issues surrounding cancer, but also – quite simply – because it's a captivating read.

Gillian Batt
DIRECTOR
Cancer Information & Support Services Division
Cancer Council NSW

# INTRODUCTION

"You've got cancer!"

The accusation is delivered sympathetically by a pretty female doctor who seems to be more upset by the news than me. I wasn't expecting this to be the reason for my pains and sleepless nights. Only that morning I had worked chest and back in the weights' room, avoiding a run because I'd been feeling strangely fatigued lately. She was still looking at me, waiting for a response, waiting for the news to sink in and decimate my strong composure, as if I was a house of straw standing in a gale-force wind. I didn't fall though, I was too proud to show her any emotion.

"Cancer? You've got to be fucking kidding me!" That's what I was thinking, but all that escapes me is a nervous laugh. How else can I react? I am 25 years old, 105 kg; I lift weights, box and play rugby in the front row. I am an Australian soldier for Christ's sake, I sure as hell cannot cry - at least not in front of a chick. I looked down at my hands, calloused from training and clenched ready to fight. But there is no-one to hit, no target to shoot and no enemy, just the pain in my hips and the shock in my head.

This was not the war I had been training for all my life. I suddenly felt hurt, betrayed by my own body. It was going to take another two weeks before I did cry, and in an airplane toilet thousands of feet above the ground my reality finally crashed. But at least I was alone and no-one saw it happen.

The next eight years were a rolling battle fought across my body and across the globe. I was going to be cut open seven times and be submitted to chemical warfare through chemotherapy. Contrary to any heroic ideal, the battle I fought was going to see me taking hits and being knocked down – injured over and over again. My only solace was going to be a determined spirit that allowed me to constantly pick myself up again, dust myself off, and get ready for the next round

I trained my body in preparation for each engagement as though I was preparing for a boxing match or battle. Strength and cardio training, cross-training, recovery sessions, mental preparation, if I was going to be forced to fight this prick I would fight him on the ground of my choosing. But this doesn't mean I didn't lose my way at times or make plenty of mistakes.

I would lose half of my nuts, a kidney, a third of my lungs and the ability to run up a flight of stairs. I would have to rely on people to shower me and wipe my arse. I would actually look forward to a 15-hour life-threatening operation just because it would mean I could evade any more chemotherapy.

Seven years later, I would then almost hope that my cancer would develop in a way that would allow my doctors to use stem-cell chemotherapy to fight it as opposed to undergoing a second 15-hour operation which would probably kill me.

"Now you do know that this is a massive operation that could kill you, Matthew?" my doctor would say. We had developed such a close relationship now that he could be frank.

"What happens if we don't operate, Doc?"

"Oh, you'll die."

"Then I guess we operate."

We guys talk about the adrenaline rush connected to riding through the barrel of an 8ft wave, screaming down the slope of a snow-covered mountain or stepping into the ring with a mountainous thug of a man. We are ultra-competitive even in the most ridiculous of gambles, anything we can find that gives us the chance to pit our skill and wits against someone or something else is fair game. Well, try calling on an operation like this sober and you'll feel a rush. Nothing makes you feel more alive than a meeting with death.

During my time off from fighting cancer, I traveled to China in an attempt to find peace and then was deployed to Iraq and Afghanistan to wage war on terrorism. I am an Alpha-male who cannot have children. I am now a walking contradiction – but at least I am still walking. Everything I thought I had and was has been challenged, but I now find myself happier than I remember being before this war. The best thing about my cancer is that it has taught me how to live better.

Cancer Sucks! It is without a doubt an absolute shit of a disease. It has all the qualities of the perfect guerilla-tactician. Just as if our body was a country and the mind was the government, cancer can infiltrate via corrupt cells and spread its filth silently. What could be considered minor ailments, illnesses or pains, are actually small raiding parties; cancer disguised and indistinguishable. When the disease is finally exposed, it is through ambush, its timing so coordinated that the nation is never left un-scarred. Once diagnosed, we suddenly find ourselves at war on all fronts and sometimes there is just no escape from its killing ground. Our red blood cells and immune system is suddenly outmatched by a marching force of single-minded and hungry malignant cells, devouring all the body's natural resources and over-running vital organs critical to survival. It advances through the lymphatic system in a similar way to the perceived communist-hordes of the Cold War era. Cancer can either decide to be swift and lethal, or lethargic and debilitating, slowly eating away until there is little left but a shadow of a once thriving and powerful nation.

But human nature has its own amazing qualities once applied to this conflict and these can be used to counter a very personal insurgency. Firstly we love a challenge! If we can look at this disease like an enemy we can fight it, as opposed to just "suffering" the effects; we are able to take command of the situation. We have allies. Doctors, nurses, scientists, family and friends, there are no strangers in the fight with cancer. In the eyes of everyone I have met during this war I have always found them pleading with me – fight on Matt, don't give up. How can a soldier deny a challenge like that?

I have always been conscious not to say that I suffer from cancer. I am not a victim of cancer, I am fighting cancer. I can take responsibility for my decisions and battle this enemy on my own grounds. The beautiful thing about being a soldier is that I can look at things in very simple ways. Regardless of whether I have cancer or not, I am going to die eventually. What is important is how I deal with this challenge; I'll always take up the fight.

Naively I used to believe that cancer afflicted old people, or those poor young kids who got leukemia. It would never happen to me. I am more likely to step on a land-mine, not get an arse-kicking from some disease. Looking back from the time of diagnosis, I have sought out and tried every viable method of cancer treatment and management. Along my journey I have undergone conventional western methods of surgery and chemotherapy, and then moved onto energetic healing, meditation, vegetarianism and fasting. I have been on turmeric and ginger tablets and even tried *Amaroli* (A more pleasant word for "urine therapy". Un-screw your face, have a drink of water, look it up on the internet and then we'll continue). I have gone on a self-discovering journey to be with Taoist monks in the mountains of China, looking for an ancient elixir. I came back to Australia only to find just as much peace surfing along Sydney's Northern beaches. Within 24 months of seriously considering becoming a pacifist monk in Asia or going to an Ashram in India, I found myself preparing to go on operational deployment in the Middle East with the Australian Defence Force. And, in that place of sand, rock and violence, a place where humanity really is not at its best, I finally started to realise some truths. Firstly, that it doesn't really matter how healthy or disease-ridden we might be, we are all just a moment away from death and we can never outrun it. Secondly, it is not the situation that defines any of us, but rather what we do to make the most of that situation. Finally, no matter whom you talk to, learn from, work for or worship, the only person that will make you truly happy in life, and eventually in death, is yourself.

It took me a while to come to the realisation that a battle against cancer can be approached in the same way as a war and in particular a counter insurgency conflict (COIN) such as Iraq or Afghanistan. Like any military operation, you will need a sound and simple strategy if you are to have any chance of success. Ask yourself now, if you have cancer, or if you were to be diagnosed; how am I going to fight it? What is my strategy? Can I live with this strategy and sustain it for the length of the fight?

Cancer is no longer just "bad luck" and I fear there will never be a "golden cure". Instead we will continue to be diagnosed and we will need to fight tooth and nail to survive. My story is about how I learnt that surviving cancer itself is only the beginning, and like a counter insurgency conflict, once diagnosed, you will never be the way same as before. Things may be better, or worse, or a combination of both. And once all the forces have pulled out, the doctors and nurses have moved on to the next battle, the battle-scars have healed and the hair has grown back, once five or twenty years have passed, a cancer survivor will always have those memories and the fear of a recurrence of the insurgency.

I think fighting hard is exactly what we should do when the doctors say those formidable words: "You have cancer." We need to rally forces and be strong. We need to be cunning and decisive and believe in ourselves.

I am very proud of this book. It is the culmination of my life's experience and my ability to deal with a very deadly disease. I am proud of how I've dealt with this personal war. I have been surrounded by very gifted specialists and loving family and friends. I cannot imagine how I would have survived this war alone, but at the same time, I alone have seen this fight through its entirety and will continue to for as long as I need to. For a disease that has taken so much from me and brought me so close to death, it has also given me the strength and confidence to embrace life so much more graciously.

This book will describe medical terms in a way that will make doctors and medical specialists cringe. I will refer to experiences that will have Defence personnel choking in protest. I am not a scientist, doctor or a brilliant officer. I am a good soldier and I am very good at surviving cancer. It seems to be my speciality.

## The Soldier (anon)

*Between the security of childhood and the senility of old age is found that
Fascinating group of humanity called the 'soldier'.*

*The soldier can be found anywhere, in love, in trouble
and always in debt. Girls love them, towns tolerate them, hotels hide them
and governments support them.*

*A soldier is laziness with a deck of cards, bravery with a tattoo, ruggedness in
uniform and defender of the world with a copy of 'playboy'. He has the brains
of a bear, the energy of a sea turtle, the slyness of a fox, the stories of a
sea-captain,
the sincerity of a liar, the aspiration of a Casanova and when he wants
something it is usually connected with leave, or and 'excused from all duties'
chit.*

*Some of his interests are girls, females, women and members of the opposite
sex. He also likes beer, booze, plonk, alcohol and ale. He likes to spend his
money on girls, beer, cards and any that he has left after pay-day, he likes to
spend foolishly.*

*No-one else could ever cram into one pocket a little black book, a packet of
crushed cigarettes, a box of matches, a picture of his girl, an old leave pass,
receipts for 'Tiger', receipts for 'Anchor', receipts for lost equipment and a deck
of cards.*

*A soldier is a magical creature. You can lock him out of your house, but not
out of your heart. You can take him off your mailing list, but not off your
mind.
He is a 'one and only', bleary-eyed bundle of worries. But all your shattered
dreams become insignificant when he looks at you and says 'Hiya, honey'!*

# THE EARLY YEARS

"I am a soldier. A warrior". This has been the way I have seen myself for as long as I can remember. I remember playing with Army-men and being the heroic soldier who runs around killing the bad guys, just like the verse in that song, "everybody wants to be a hero". Who was that by?

I know this is a phase that most boys go through while they are growing up, but I didn't grow out of it. In my early teens I started Martial Arts training at the PCYC club in Dubbo, country New South Wales, an "old school" club with one hall shared by kids learning Kung Fu and others learning ballet; playing basketball and staff also setting up for Friday night bingo. I originally started these Kung Fu classes after copping a fair few beatings! I was arrogant then and this arrogance could be described as misplaced as I had very little to back it up. I was pretty plump and very uncoordinated. So the reality of me becoming a hardened warrior who would sweep all adversaries before him like a vengeful tsunami was a bit of a fantasy. Even as I began my Kung Fu classes you couldn't say I was naturally gifted. In true Matt Carr unco-ordinated fashion, I failed the grading to get my green belt (the 3rd belt on the ladder). All the people who had started around the same time, including my best mate, Todd, passed. Along with the hidings I had received by those who were offended by round, big-eared and loud mouthed smart-arses, this early failure was a pretty massive blow to my fledgling ego.

But something happened or should I say *emerged* that was to become maybe my single biggest quality that would to save me from the most lethal enemy I was ever going to face. I wouldn't say I was angry, as deep down I knew at the time I was not very good (my father, a Vietnam vet, regularly observed that if I was to go to war I would walk on every land mine laid due to my clumsiness!) And anyway, who was I going to blame? And if I did blame someone, what was I going to do about it? I couldn't fight! Instead, I became aggressively determined to prove, to myself more than anyone else, that I would get what I wanted (and at that time all I wanted was to get that next bloody belt). At home I started doing sit-ups and push-ups every night and Dad put up a punching bag in the garage. I had a family friend, who was into body building and worked at the local gym, draw me up a weights program.

By the time the next grading came around six months later, I actually went for a double-grading and attempted to claim two belts in one exam. I made it through both and was back to the same level as my peers! Although I was still pretty average as far as Kung Fu and co-ordination went, I had learnt a very special lesson about what I was capable of. I was a very average, ordinary person, with no special ninja gifts that would hurtle me to glory. But I did have a very special trait; determination. From that initial success came some new-found confidence (not that my wife would say that I needed any more), but this time I knew how to apply this confidence. I went on to do whatever I could to get to my goal of black belt and in the process develop some much needed co-ordination and body-awareness. I even secretly went to African dancing classes being run by an Afro-American guy I met at the gym. This was an attempt to become more co-ordinated (and because he promised me that blokes who could dance well, always got the girls!) I was the only guy in the class and was going pretty well, until my dad found out and started asking some scary questions about my sexuality. By 18 I had my black belt in both Kung Fu and Judo (thanks to a year as an exchange student in Japan) and I had earned them. I was finally on the road to being that soldier and going to that war I had always imagined I was destined for.

The trip to Japan came about at the end of year 10 when I won a scholarship to go on exchange to Tokyo for 12 months. The scholarship was funded by the NSW and Japanese governments and run by an organisation called AFS. To get it, I had to go to a number of interviews and selection panels. The result was an all expenses trip. I was 16 and this was the first time I would be away from my family for such a long time. Although I'd traveled overseas a few times with my family, this seemed like my first big adventure. It would be a chance for me to learn a language, improve my martial arts and get away from all that was normal in my life. This was a time to start exploring myself as much as I was going out to explore the world.

As a young man, independence was also growing inside me. My mum has always said that I went away a boy and came back a man. I won't go into too much detail about that trip and some of the adventures I had over there; that is another story completely. However, I do recall having a difficult time being accepted into a very traditional Japanese family and feeling extremely lonely. This was made worse by the passing of my Grandfather half-way through the year. I remember the phone call from Mum quite clearly, and the emotionless Japanese faces of my host family staring back at me as I burst into tears in front of them. Japanese was a hard enough language for me to learn as it was. Strangely enough, "My grandfather has just died. The funeral is in a week and I would like to go home now please", was not one of the phrases I had learnt to put together at that time. I finally got that message across with the help of an English-Japanese translation book, some sign language and a box of tissues. Mum and Dad convinced me not to return home and I was confronted by the thought of a very lonely and cold six months in this foreign land, not the adventure I had imagined. For the second time in my life I was saved by that strengthening trait of determination. I filled my time with Judo and Kempo training as well as some very enjoyable under-age drinking sessions in *Roppongi* (the night club centre of Tokyo). As difficult as loneliness is, there is a peace and strength that can be found in it. In that year in Japan

I realised that you can be lonely, without being alone. You can achieve and accomplish a lot when there are no distractions from parents, siblings and peers. Within 10 years I was also going to learn the flip-side of that lesson. Whereas you can be surrounded by all the friends and family in your world, and still feel very lonely and helpless, and totally dependent on who and what are around you (especially a wife, parents and the love of a good sister).

I returned home to Australia with a pony tail, reeking of red wine and unrecognisable to my family! I remember walking out of customs and seeing my mum, dad and sister standing there waiting for me. As I walked up to them I realised that I was blocking their view as they peered around me to continue looking.. I felt that change inside me as well. I was now quite independent and had actually matured so much that I settled back into school and started studying and doing homework, which came as a shock to teachers and parents alike. But I had a goal now and a plan. Without realising it, I had a strategy.

The Army was now a realistic option for me (and my ninja skills were coming along nicely too). I set about applying for a scholarship to the Australian Defence Force Academy (ADFA). This is the Defence Force's University where you get a degree as a prelude to becoming an Officer in the Australian Defence Force. I am by no means an academic, but now that I had the discipline to study, my marks were improving and obtaining the scholarship meant that I was assured entry (providing I received the required university entrance marks). The only real sacrifice this cost me was my much-loved pony tail, which came off after the first of the vetting interviews when a Major made some comment about radical hairstyles. I got a good score in my Higher School Certificate and in

January of 1996, I was finally marching into the Army.

I took to the military with relative ease. As usual I was never as good as I thought I was, but my determination paid off and kept me coasting along. The Army is one of those institutions where arrogance is actually encouraged, to an extent, and at the same time this institution teaches you some much needed humility. For as good as you think you are, there is always someone better, or higher in the pecking order, to keep you in line. It is a very stoic, rugged environment and the showing of emotions is discouraged from the very beginning. I was fortunate to always be surrounded by the very best of mates and people that were very honorable and loyal. I knew my mates to be of the highest quality and we were all relatively hard and strong personalities. We were officers and soldiers in the Army (I had some friends who were to be officers in the RAAF and Navy, but they were never as hard as us Army guys!) and together we grew into a mould which came with responsibility and discipline. However, one thing that has stayed with me through my cancer ordeal was my surprise at realising just how loving and supportive the military brethren can be. As my cancer grew inside me, so did the concern and support I received from these mates. A war, it seems, doesn't just have to be fought over borders, or between people in order to encapsulate an *espirit de corps* and the mateship that is so renowned in our Defence Force.

I graduated from ADFA in 1998 and by the end of the following year I was marching out from the Royal Military College, Duntroon. I had filled out a bit and was co-ordinated enough to play in the front row of our Rugby Union team (true rugby players will know this requires a hell of a lot of co-ordination). I also graduated as the captain of our boxing squad. I loved the Army lifestyle, image and ethos. I thrived on the aggression and respect it commanded and was proud whenever it was commented that I "looked (or acted) like an Army guy", although a lot of times I don't think this was intended as a compliment.

So by the time I marched out from Duntroon, I felt as though the world was at my feet. The old phrase "ten-foot tall and bulletproof" explains perfectly my exhilaration on that graduation day. I was a little over 6 foot, 100kgs, very fit and healthy and soon to be in command of, in my view, the best soldiers in the world – Australian soldiers. East Timor was gaining its independence during this time so naturally I, and every other soldier in the Army, was setting my sights on one of the few major operations Australia has been involved in since the Vietnam War. The last thing on my mind was illness.

However, before the government was handed such a primed and lethal military tool such as myself, I was posted to Puckapunyal in Victoria for my Regimental Officers Basic Course. I had graduated as a Cavalry Officer in the Royal Australian Armoured Corps. This term was repeated extensively throughout bars and night clubs along the Australian East coast as I thought it to be the sexiest introduction EVER, and surely no lady could refuse advances from a warrior who fights for her democratic freedom. (I think I may have still been stuck in the cold war era). I, along with the rest of my cohort, would be posted to Puckapunyal for the next six months honing our troop leading and tactical skills before going to our Regiments.

By the end of 2001 things were going pretty smoothly. I had been posted to the 2nd Cavalry Regiment in Darwin and was loving my chosen profession, although I hadn't yet served in a war zone. I had missed out on going to Timor but I am pretty sure this was because the Australian Government did not want to escalate the fragile peace we had gained over there with Indonesia by sending in a weapon such as myself. This was pretty disappointing. but within a few months I would realise that it was definitely a blessing in disguise.

I had now been to Singapore and the US for training. In six years since joining the Army I had already moved three times and was set for a re-posting down to Wagga Wagga to work at the Army Recruit Training Centre. Darwin had been special to me though. My mum had since relocated up there and so I had a homebase on weekends. She and my step-dad, Gordon, lived in Parap, a suburb close to the centre of town, so it was the perfect location for me and the boys to make raids into the nightclubs and bars two - five nights a week. And in true motherly fashion, breakfast was always ready when we dragged ourselves home. In between these social attacks on the local, and the backpacking female population, I would go fishing with Gordon for that elusive barramundi, or mud crabbing. These were good days. I was still invincible and had even managed to not get arrested or married (although there were a few close calls). I would actually like to take this opportunity to thank the Darwin, Dubbo, Canberra and Seymour police for their understanding, compassion and patience during the last decade.

I was living the ultimate young man's life with a job I loved, earning a terribly insufficient income, playing rugby and boxing through the week and enjoying a healthy drinking habit. Now if I could just get some pain killers for this weird hip pain that kept coming back, I could claim a perfect life…

# WAGGA WAGGA

I arrived in Wagga in late 2001. Although I had loved living in Darwin, I was still very restless and any change was good. Having grown up in Dubbo meant I was quite at home in country New South Wales. I was keen to rent a house with a backyard and get a dog. The posting to Wagga meant that I would not be "out bush" on exercise and war games as much so I would be able to better care for a little canine companion.

In a Regiment (the term used to describe a combat unit

of anything up to about 500 soldiers) it's not uncommon for soldiers to be away up to six months of the year on various exercises, even without a commitment to any overseas operations. For the journey south I traveled through Alice Springs and the centre of Australia to Adelaide. To do this drive justice, you need at least a week, so time can be spent exploring the Red Centre and enjoying the unique personalities of some of the townships along the way. I was in a hurry so I did it in two.

I had advertised at some of the backpacking places in Darwin for anyone who wanted a free ride down to Adelaide. This idea had two motives. One was to keep me company along the way, and the second was to meet up with some lovely Swedish backpacker and talk to her about our varying cultures. I had received no calls until the day before I was due to depart. To my disappointment the backpacker was a young British lad, but I decided that some company was better than none. As it turned out this guy slept the whole way to Alice Springs, after having a massive night out and decided to stay in Alice for a few days and check it out. So that was the thanks I got from trying to be a good diplomat for our country!

The only thing bothering me the whole trip was this crazy little pain I kept getting in my right hip. I had been to the Regimental Medical Officer in Darwin and he had suggested that I had strained it either in a Rugby game or weight training. He had given me some anti-inflammatory drugs and that seemed to do the job for a while, but this annoying little pain kept coming back and had even started keeping me up for a few hours each night.

I arrived in Wagga with a week to find a place to live and then begin work at the recruit training centre. A good mate who was also posted to Kapooka was on his way down and we had decided to get a "bach-pad" together. I found a very ordinary older-style house in the Glenfield estate. It hadn't been greatly loved but sported a large enclosed backyard, perfect for two guys, a dog and little interest in housekeeping.

At my new job I had a sergeant and three corporals, all of who were really good men and I could tell we were going to have a pretty good year. The sergeant in particular had a deep, gruff, bellowing voice that carried authority like only a sergeant can. On the exterior he had a personality that matched his voice, but a scratch under the surface showed a kind, well-meaning man who only had the best interest of his staff and recruits at heart.

It was during these first few weeks that I decided to go to the doctor again and get this pain checked out. Another trait of being a soldier is bravado and the instinctive habit not to show any pain. I am not sure if this is from watching too many war movies where guys like Rambo pull shrapnel out of their sides and then cauterise the wound with gun powder (*Rambo III*), or just the whole male ocker thing. Either way, I didn't make it a habit of going to doctors and wasn't impressed that I had to go back again. But the pain was starting to get worse. Since Darwin it had moved into both hips and was starting to creep into my lower back. The anti-inflammatory drugs were no longer having an effect, and I wasn't sleeping well. To make matters worse it was starting to affect my drinking and social life.

It is probably a good time to explain a little method I'm going to use throughout this book. I am going to give "call-signs" to certain identities throughout the story (call-signs are nicknames used in the Army especially during radio transmissions to identify one-another without using personal names, which may be detected by the enemy using electronic counter measures). This is to avoid any embarrassment or legal issues that may result from my comments. So the first doctor I met I am going call Dr Misdiagnosis. This GP had been in the Army for most of his life and I assume that by the time I went to him, was nearing the end of his professional career and capability. Dr Misdiagnosis was very quick to let me know that I was suffering from some back ailment; it was hard for him to lock down the exact cause but that it had probably occurred during weight training. He said a lot of people get back pain and apart from some drugs and some rest there wasn't much else he could do I would have to put up with it and get over it. He did write me a referral to see the physiotherapist which was very nice of him. I had no reason to doubt this man. After all he was the doctor and I was young and fit. This would all clear up in time and I'd also be able to get a few massages from the physio – no problems.

The Army physio – Ro, was a great girl and she proceeded to give me some core exercises to do each day, a massage and treatment with a really funky electro-device. You place these pads on an area of your body and it sends little electric pulses into your muscles. This seemed to have a bit of an impact so I got addicted to it pretty quickly. But I think it was just masking the pain. I went to Ro for about three to four weeks and to the surprise of both of us, the pain was still there. Alarmingly it was actually getting worse. Christmas was approaching and this was a busy time. We were training recruits through the Christmas period and had to compound the training as they would get Christmas day off and we needed to catch up on the lessons that had been missed. It was also busy as even though we were working each day; time still had to be given to drinking and socialising.

Around New Year's was going to be very special for me too as it was time to drive up to Mittagong and pick up my boy Hector. At eight weeks Hector, a light tan bullmastiff, was 5kgs of head and paws and a ball of slobbering affection. I had big plans for him, which included acting as an intimidating mascot for my platoon, taking me running, and using him to talk to girls.

Again life was frustratingly close to being perfect, but one night just after New Year's Eve I had to drive myself to the medical centre on base doubled over in pain. I was getting some serious pain through my abdomen. It was about 3am and I was in trouble. I had never experienced this kind of consistent, throbbing pain. The nurses dosed me up on some strong pain killers and I got a few hours sleep. The next day I went to my Officer in Command (a Major in rank), and told him what had been going on in the last few weeks. I explained that I was now averaging about three hours sleep a night and had even had some problems doing the physical training with the recruits. A few days earlier Ro had raised her concerns with me as she suspected something more seriously wrong with me than just muscular back pain. My boss gave me the week off to rest and sort out the problem. He told me to go back to Dr Misdiagnosis and get checked out again.

Looking back now I knew that something was wrong, really wrong. But in that young, ignorant stage in my life I put the shutters up. I had been told by the Dr again that I was just aggravating the injury by working and training, and that he could find nothing wrong with me. Although every other doctor I have been involved with since has been more than exceptional, this initial experience taught me a valuable lesson. Listen to my body. Doctors are human, just like the rest of us, and are subject to making mistakes, passing judgment and having prejudice. It is easy to forget that it is we who are in command of our bodies and ultimately we have to take the responsibility and bear the burden when things go wrong. I found out soon after that Ro had approached him about my condition. She was concerned that her treatment was having no effect and that she believed that I had a more serious condition. His response was that he believed I was probably just malingering. (Cheers, Doc.)

I went back to work after a week off in no better condition. I was now lucky to get two hours sleep a night. I would lie in bed trying to sleep until the pain got unbearable. I would run a hot bath and lie in it for another hour or two, pop a few pain killers and pass out until 6am. I was eating significantly less and was even off alcohol! Things were bad ... I was no longer training and could not even walk more than 100 metres without stopping and trying to stretch my back and ease the pain.

Around this time I experienced something very strange and frightening indeed. I had just stepped out of the shower one morning and noticed that one of my testes was swollen to twice its normal size. Now usually I would throw in a very crude innuendo right about here but I don't want to detract from the gravity of the situation. For around a year, I had experienced a tender teste. This never seemed to stop me from performing a favorite pass-time, and it was never bad enough to warrant concern, it was just tender. I remembered having a cousin who once had a twisted teste and I thought that maybe it was that. One of the most stupid things I have done in my life (and I will admit that there have been a few) was not getting this checked out. But these were my family jewels and only the privileged were granted access, and definitely not some strange doctor with latex gloves. The swelling went down within an hour or so, and I thought nothing more about it. I was in too much pain to worry about it.

Then a minor miracle occurred (this may sound dramatic but the timing really could not have been better). Ro rang me to let me know that Dr Misdiagnosis was going away on leave for a few weeks and there was a replacement! She suggested I make an appointment immediately and get a second opinion. I was waiting outside the office by that afternoon. Dr Honey welcomed me into the office, if she hadn't been sporting a wedding ring, and if I hadn't been in so much pain, I would have been much more charming towards her indeed. Dr Honey listened to my symptoms and prodded around a bit. I don't recall mentioning the swollen teste incident as I was sure that it wasn't important, but either way she was onto this like a reconnaissance soldier to a blood trail. She immediately booked me in for some x-rays and scans. The results came in within a few days and she was a little non-committal, she told me she was going to book me in for a biopsy. A what? She explained the procedure as having a pretty large needle inserted into you to draw some tissue out for examination. I think she may have suspected something then but didn't mention what she was looking for. Oh well, she's the doctor and taking a lot more interest in me than the other *"specialist"*. So off I was for my first biopsy which I can say, was shit. The specialist used a local anesthetic which helped out a bit but I was in so much pain now that even lying on my belly for more than a few minutes was soul destroying. The biopsy must have taken about 45minutes but it felt like four or five hours.

Dr Honey – "Hi Matthew, come in and please take a seat."

She seemed a little concerned. It almost looked like she had been crying. What was going on?

Me – "Hi Doc, you got some news for me I hope. Have we found an answer to all this?"

There was a moment of hesitation on her part. And a quickening of the pulse on mine. What could this be? It must be pretty big shit if she is choosing her words so carefully. I wonder if I will get out of organising the annual local area officers' ball that my boss had stabbed me with a few weeks ago....

Dr Honey – "Matthew, have you ever heard of Non-Hodgekin's disease?"

Me – "Na, what's that?"

Dr Honey – "It's a type of cancer".

Me (very nervously) – "Ha ha ha ... what do you mean Cancer? Can it be fixed?"

Dr Honey – "It can be treated..."

Me (cutting in) – "How long?" Six months? Will the Army still employ me?"

The questions were starting to flood my brain but I really did need to control myself. After all I was a soldier and needed to keep calm, especially in front of a woman. Dr Honey went on to explain that it was not yet confirmed and I needed a few more tests done. However, what was certain was that I was seriously ill and would be taking time off work. Someone else was going to have to organise the officers' ball.

"Just tell me what has to be done to get better, Doc, and I'll do it".

I still had no real idea of what was going on, but people didn't die from cancer unless they were really old. This will just slow me down for six months. Nic (my house mate) would have to do his training for Special Forces on his own. I walked out of the medical centre and wasn't too sure what to do. I decided to call my best friend Todd. Todd and I have been mates since we were about four years old. I had a sister, but Todd is as close to a brother as I could ask, and he is a good listener. I didn't need anyone to tell me what to do, I just needed to talk to someone.

Todd (answering his mobile) – "hello Mate, what's going on?"

Me (very casually) – "hey mate. Just thought I'd ring and tell you something. You know how I've been feeling not so well lately, well it looks like I might have cancer."

Todd – "Oh."

Me – "Yeah but it should be fine. The Doc said it can be treated and I should be right in six months."

I don't keep a journal, and a lot of my memories have been blurred by time, distraction and pain, but I do remember quite clearly these two conversations with the doctor and Todd. It is like a cellular memory. My body knew that I was in a bit of shit and wanted to store this moment away for the future (in case perhaps I decided to write a book). I hung up on Todd quickly. He didn't get the chance to say much, even if he did have the right words to say.

Now back to business, the Doc had some more tests for me and said that I needed to finish up work pretty quickly. I had a lot to organise and very little time to explain all this stuff to my boss and colleagues (not that I knew how to explain what was going on anyway). First stop was my boss. He couldn't have been more understanding and it felt weird that he seemed so concerned. I started to explain that I wouldn't be able to complete the training of my current platoon and I wouldn't be able to organise the ball (I will admit there was some relief there). He told me not to worry about the damn ball; I should go home and call my family. (I hadn't even thought of my family at that stage.) They could wait. That would make everything too serious. I went to my sergeant. I felt embarrassed telling him what was happening; telling him that I was going to be too sick to continue working and march out the current platoon. It made me feel weak. He must have sensed it as his response was perfect. He simply listened and at the end of it all, with no emotion, simply asked "Is there anything I can do for you sir?" No, I was fine. But I could feel the sincerity in the offer and appreciated it.

When you tell someone you have cancer, it is not just you and your welfare that the people you are telling are thinking about. Cancer is now so infused in our lives and society that more people than not have been deeply affected by it. The emotions that are stirred in your audience are massive and varied. Cancer not only affects the patient, but the patient's family and friends. And if you have ever had to sit by and watch a loved one waste away helplessly before your eyes, you would agree that it is not an experience you would wish upon anyone. I had no idea that my boss or my Sergeant may have had a parent, or loved one that had perhaps died from cancer. When people were quiet when I told them that I had cancer, it was often not because they were as ignorant as me as to what it all meant, but instead it may have reminded them of their experience with the disease. Their concern could also be fear and sorrow. In fact, those that are less affected by cancer are the ones who talk more about it.

I decided not to tell my family straight away. I needed answers to all the questions that would surely come up after such an announcement. The one person I did call was Gordon, Mum's husband. I knew I had to tell him before Mum so he could be prepared to deal with the reaction. At that time I remember thinking that he was a pretty stoic man and would listen without getting too concerned. Again ignorant me didn't consider that he had lost his first wife to cancer. But true to Gordon's character, he just listened and did what I asked of him without betraying any of his own fears or thoughts. In fact I got a similar response from my other mates. I wonder if it was due to the way I told them, or the fact that the news stirred feelings inside them which they were unsure how to deal with, or a combination of both.

In a few days I was sitting back in Dr Honey's office. My respect for her was growing with every conversation. She was right into organisational mode now and that's the way I liked it. It's what I was used to, and the familiarity was comforting. The emotion could come later. There had been a little bit of confusion with some of the test results, and I had been to get an ultra-sound on my scrotum the day before. Now this ultra-sound thing was supposed to be for pregnant chicks so I didn't know what this was all about, except for the fact that they should really warm that lube up before smearing it all over a bloke's package (and those rooms are really cold). So now I was sitting in this office again ready for whatever answers the Doc had for me.

There was good news and bad news (ok, this is sounding a bit like a movie). I didn't have Hodgekinsons Lymphoma or Non-Hodgekinsons Lymphoma, apparently this was the good news. Hurray for me. I had no idea but listened with what I hoped was a look of sage intelligence on my face. "It's Testicular Cancer though, and it is quite advanced." Right, finally an answer, but what does that mean? The advanced state of the cancer was the reason why I had found a lump starting to grow from the bottom of my neck that week, sort of like I had the mumps, but in the wrong place. Dr Honey went on to explain that testicular cancer is most common in young active and fit males. Well it was good that she had noticed I was young and active. I hadn't worked on my biceps for her not to, but what is this "common" thing? I had never heard of it.

"Testicular cancer is quite responsive to chemotherapy," she continued, and most patients go on to lead long and active lives. (This was sounding good. Should be a piece of cake.) However, once this type of cancer spreads into the lymphatic system, it becomes very aggressive and moves quickly through the body and into major organs. Time it would seem was no longer on my side. "One other thing, you will need to have the teste removed." Ok now I was getting worried, what the hell did that mean?

The plan was to wrap everything up in Wagga and get on a plane to Darwin to start treatment within the week. I had told Mum and Dad on the phone and asked Mum if I could stay with them during the treatment. I played down the seriousness, not really out of bravado, but out of stubborn ignorance. I really didn't know much of what was going on, and didn't see myself as being in that much peril. The doctors had explained it to me, but most of that went straight over my head. Medical talk…

A few days before I left Ro came to see me. We talked

about how everything now made sense and how she had known there was something else going on. She also handed me a book.

Ro – "Have you ever heard of Lance Armstrong, the bike rider?"

Me – "Na, I'm a boxer and rugby player. Bikes don't interest me".

She handed me the book and explained that he had gone through exactly what I was going through and it would be good to read it. I thanked her and she gave me a hug. A bit emotional, and in uniform at the time, but I thought "what the heck" and hugged her back.

The night before I left for Darwin, a very special friend of mine from Dubbo, who had been working in Canberra, came to see me. Michelle and I had gone through high school together and no matter how hard I had tried, she always refused my advances. Besides this, we were still very close friends, and maybe it was that she knew me too well to ever be tricked by my charms. Michelle drove in, and I set up a bed for her in the lounge room. I remember thinking that this was the first time she had come to visit since I had arrived in Wagga and that maybe she was really concerned about what was going on. We talked into the night and she asked how my folks had been with the news. I had told Mum and Dad, but I still hadn't thought how they were going. Mum was happy that I was coming up to her so she could do the mother thing. Even though I am a soldier, I am still only human, and what guy doesn't let his mum fuss over him when he is sick. Dad was customarily calm about it all. He is a pretty logical and matter-of-fact guy, who isn't big on the whole emotionally expressive thing. In the few times we had spoken though, he seemed to have more and more knowledge about my disease. It turns out that he started doing some in-depth research on the computer regarding this cancer, and that alone should have been a good enough sign that he was worried. Dad wasn't really into computers.

Michelle drove me out to the airport the next morning in the ute. Hector was in the back. The ute was staying down south, but my boy was coming up north with me. He was still only little at this stage and so didn't need a big cage. I had dosed him up with some sleeping tablets earlier on and these were starting to take effect. He looked at me with sleepy but confused eyes, and I wonder if I looked back at him with the same expression. I had a slight shimmer that I was going on an adventure, but also a feeling of dread, and what was this other feeling? Fear?

# THE PLANE FLIGHT

The plane flight was a lot more significant a trip than I had originally intended. I got a big hug from Michelle. These hugs were starting to come thick and fast and I was starting to appreciate them. At least I wasn't in uniform this time so I could relax and enjoy it more. I hopped onto the plane at the same time as they were loading Hector on. He was snoozing by now and I was a little envious of him. My mind was starting to race with questions I had no answer for, and some sleep would have been a welcome distraction. I had anticipated this nervousness and brought along something to take my mind off things – a book. As the wheels lifted off from Wagga Wagga, I opened to page 1 of Lance Armstrong's *it's not about the bike*, and tried to get as comfortable as possible for a long trip. Although I was still in pain with my back, I don't remember the pain being as bad as before diagnosis. My mind was so preoccupied trying to process everything that was going on that these pains took a back seat. In all my haste to get everything organised I had also failed to realise that the flights the administration staff at the medical centre booked for me included a four-hour stopover in Sydney. This meant that the trip to Darwin was going to take about nine hours!

As soon as I started reading things went bad. In the early parts I began to find a connection with old Lance. But if you have read his book, you will recall that quite quickly he gets into the details of how bad his situation was. Reading his book at this time felt like the worst thing I could have done. I was alone, surrounded by strangers, in transit to have my nut removed, and God knows what else, and now I was reading exactly what was going to happen to me over the next few months. The information from the book was not really any different from what the doctors had told me, but reading about this guy going through it made it more personal. It made my situation real. This was no adventure or a chance to get some fishing done on a holiday. This was serious, and it was going to be a war that was more dangerous than any I could have wished to go to, because in this war, I was going to be a casualty, no matter how quick or strong or smart I was (not that the last one ever really was a good asset for me). I started to feel a little like our ANZACs did at Lone Pine in Gallipoli, waiting to go over those trenches and into the firing line of machine guns, only my enemy was firing at me with machince guns loaded with little cancer bullets. Those four hours waiting in Sydney I think were among the worst moments of my whole ordeal. I couldn't go anywhere to escape that book and what it was telling me. The more I read it, the more I thought to myself – "I'm fucked."

After what seemed an eternity the plane was ready to board for Darwin. About an hour into the flight I hit rock bottom. I had to put the book down and go very hurriedly to the toilet where for the first time I broke down in tears. Things were starting to hit home and it was all Lance's fault! And Ro's for giving me that book. And all those doctors who had found things wrong with me. I sat in that little toilet a couple of thousand feet above Australia and was finally comforted by that little spark of determination that I knew I could always rely on. To use a bit of Army talk, I was now decisively engaged with the enemy. Meaning well and truly involved in the fight when your only real options are to fight through or retreat and in doing so take some heavy losses (in the Australian Army we never retreat. Though at times we may conduct a tactical withdrawal). In my case there was only one option and that was to fight through.

I decided I was not going to read any more of that book until I was through the worst of whatever lay ahead. I needed to draw up my own battle plan. I looked out the window and down into nothing for the remaining three hours and tried to steel my resolve.

This flight was more than just me going up to Darwin to start treatment. Metaphorically, this was me departing the relatively normal and sheltered life I had lived up until now, with all its ignorance, bigotry and stereotypes, and going on a journey leading to an unknown destination. The plane finally touched down in Darwin and as I walked out of the barriers I immediately saw my mum and Gordon waiting for me. And without being able to control myself, and for the second time that night, I broke down in tears. But this time it felt a bit different, a little more comforting, as I was in the arms of my mum. I finally realised I had the support of a loving family and that I didn't have to go through this alone. In the years to come, I was going to learn that there is nothing tough about trying to deal with such a challenge on my own. Also, I was going to learn how important it is to allow family and friends to help as much as they can.

I finally began to realise that I had some excellent and loyal allies in this upcoming battle. I was going to need more. I was going to meet more, but this realisation was a very good start.

# DARWIN

In Darwin they say, "When you are in pain, you get on a plane." However, a very cunning Chinese general, named Sun Tsu, a few thousand years ago also said:

"Conformation of the ground is of the greatest assistance in battle. Therefore, virtues of a superior general are to estimate the enemy situation and to calculate distances and the degree of difficulty of the terrain so as to control victory", in other words "If you have to do battle, do it on the ground of your choosing."

And so, with a very real and lethal threat of cancer marching up from my right testicle and sweeping away all immune system defenses my body could muster, I was being forced into a corner and I was in need of some outside assistance. I decided that this battle was going to be fought in the North. In the short but very torrid week since my diagnosis, I had been questioned by a few of my family and friends regarding my decision to go to Darwin. On the surface the thought of going back to the old stomping ground and going fishing whilst on chemo was very attractive. After all, hadn't Dr Honey said a little over six months and I'll be fine again? Or had that been how I had heard it? How bad could this treatment be? At a deeper level, and only realising it slightly, I needed to be home, and no matter how tough and trained a killer is, he needs his mum when he is sick. The level of treatment I was going to receive (which I had no idea about), was second priority to my feeling safe and comfortable. Looking back, and knowing then what I know now, I would not have changed that decision. In any war an army needs a base that is close to the front line, but safe and secure enough for its forces to withdraw back to for rest and consolidation. I believe a very big factor in my ability to handle, and recover, from the chemo and surgeries I had in Darwin was the strength and stability I drew from having a very good Forward Operating Base (FOB) - home. In the coming months I was going to realise that the medical support I received in Darwin was about as good as I could have wished for in any other major city in Australia, or the world, and this was due mainly to the staff.

So after a very embarrassing break down in the middle of Darwin airport, and a quick look around to make sure no one I knew was around and had seen this spectacle, we headed home. A quick stop at the freight area ensured Hector that he had not been forgotten and he looked as though he had enjoyed his trip a lot more than I had. There was adventure in his eyes that was contagious, and so he helped to rid me of some of the fears that had started to grow within me during the flight.

There was no respite to the tempo that had been set since my first diagnosis. It had been roughly a week since the "you have cancer" line had been fired at me, but it actually felt like a month. Looking back I know there was a certain amount of shock still in my system. Appointments had been made for the day after my arrival, and first on the list was Dr Serious. This man had been referred to me by the doctors in Wagga and I don't care how good he apparently was, breaking a smile on this guy was going to be tough. In hindsight I believe a better nickname to be Dr Sincere, but this was going to take about six months to discover.

Dr Sincere started throwing around a lot of terminology, explanations, statistics and needles. I was prodded and probed, and apparently from results of tests done in Wagga, I had about a 70 percent chance of recovery. But Dr Sincere was also very much Dr Thorough, and so I went through not only new tests but also another round of ones already done. Now I am not much of a guy for statistics but hearing that I had 70 percent chance of recovering meant that there was also a 30 percent of not recovering! Not recovering was not part of my strategy for this particular battle, so I ignored the stats and instead resolved to try and get this guy to lighten up.

Throughout that first day Mum was with me, always with a determined look of support. This was going to be a face that in the following years would be welcomed, scorned, resented, but always loved. She took me home and drew me a hot bath. Even though I was in the tropics, a hot bath was the only temporary relief for the constant throbbing pain in my back, and this cancer was continuing its advance.

My memories of these days are vivid. I remember almost all of the medical appointments, conversations, dealings with doctors and nurses. I can remember the smell of Darwin hospital, one that will still make me nauseous today, as my mind connects it to chemo. But I remember very little of my down time at home. My thoughts and feelings in between hospital trips are lost and overwhelmed by those events my mind found more important to lock away. I couldn't take Hector for any walks, as I was in too much pain, and the look I received from him for this was almost as painful as the tumour in my guts. I do remember Mum always pulled over at a bakery and bought me a meat pie, something I have always had a weakness for.

It was a day or so until we returned to the hospital for the test results. By coincidence, or perhaps not, Dr Sincere began to use military terminology to describe how the operation would proceed. The results had shown that my adversary was on the move and advancing more rapidly than everyone had realised. In soldiers' language – these guys are coming over the hill, right fucking now! My good doctor told me that this was changing my odds to a 50 per-cent chance of recovery. Luckily I was still preoccupied with my ambition to make this guy smile, otherwise I don't think I would have liked what he was saying. Enough intelligence for one day, it was time to go home and rest. Tomorrow would be the pre-operation appointment. As quickly as everything was moving, there was still this waiting game that had to play out.

My pre-operation appointment was a very surreal experience. Mum and I were greeted by Dr Sincere and were led into one of his consulting rooms. To my surprise there were two young people there. We were introduced to his shadows for the day – two medical students named; Mr Young and Ms Young-and-female. Dr Sincere got straight down to business describing how he intended to remove my right testicle. This scenario would have been a lot more realistic if I was speaking to a father whose daughter I had left broken hearted, in fact I had prepared myself for such an encounter. This guy was actually going to do it, and I had never even met Ms Young-and-female! Mum and I retained our composure as the technical jargon drifted through our ears.

"Now would you like me to put a prosthetic one in?"

"A what?" – I was shocked back into the discussion by the unexpected question.

"A prosthetic testicle. It will make you look normal"

"A fake nut?"

I had never really considered this particular implication of my disease until this moment. Did I want to look normal? Wasn't I already normal? Of course not, I was soon going to be a "one-nut-wonder", a "euno" - half way to eunuch! Since that day there have been many times that I have day dreamed of the potential party tricks I could have "pulled-off" with a secret synthetic testicle to squeeze, crush or twist. But in my haste I said no. I didn't feel right about hiding what I was about to go through. Anyway, my arrogance was robust enough to handle a missing nut. I was still lost in my thoughts over this latest revelation when Dr Sincere stopped talking, stood up and asked for me to follow him into the examination area. He asked Mum to wait for a moment and we proceeded to go in, along with Mr Young and Ms Young-and-female.

"Please take off your pants and hop up on the bed." It was not really a request and I was confronted by that serious face again. In fact there were three serious faces and a rapidly blushing one. Dr Sincere wanted to examine the culprit testicle and this was indeed a good opportunity for his med students to get some "hands-on experience."Now I have been guilty in the past of dropping my pants for an audience, usually to the song "eagle rock" at about 3am with a bunch of defence mates and a bottle of bourbon under the belt. In the clarity of soberness however, I was thinking that I did not have that much to flaunt, although by now, with the insistence of a little cancer, I was hefting a pretty sizable package, albeit slightly lop-sided.

So here I am, lying on my back, pants around my ankles, with three strangers inspecting my right nut. Where do I look? If I close my eyes I might look too relaxed and comfortable. If I stare at my "handlers" it could be mistaken as forward. I opted for the passive, a blank stare at the ceiling, making sure not to have my hands behind my head while noting the variations in hand-temperature. All the things I could have said in those moments were relayed to me by Gordon that night when I was re-telling the story. Even Mum, who was in focused, organisational mode, was having a hard time stifling the chuckles.

48 hours later I was slowly waking up from a groggy hangover of general anesthetic and feeling half the man I had been before going to sleep. Dr Sincere told me that the operation had been a success......not sure if I could agree with him on that. In comparison to all the operations I have had

since then, this one was easy. On the first day of my recovery I was greeted by my sister who had flown up to surprise me, as well as my dad. The troops were arriving thick and fast now whether I liked it or not. It was good to have them around, although it seemed that conversation always centred on my missing nut. Some of the boys from the barracks turned up as well. In true fashion they had slipped a six-pack of beers past the on-duty nurse and in a perverse show of mateship, we proceeded to have a drink while inspecting my renovations. Their concern was hidden by a casual humour and genuine curiosity as to how my nut had been taken out. This made it easier for me to accept what had just happened.

I was out of hospital within a day or so. Although riddled with cancer, my fitness and youth allowed me to recover quickly from the surgery. I had just had my first skirmish with the enemy and the taste of victory was in my mouth. In this war, up until now, it had been very one-sided.

I had no time to recover. No time for a victory party. Dr Sincere had booked me into the sperm clinic to get a sample before proceeding with chemo. Ok now this was getting out of control! Two weeks ago I had been diagnosed with cancer. Two days ago I had just had one of my nuts removed, and now they were asking me to sit down with a very current issue of Penthouse and go for gold! I really wasn't feeling sexy, but hey I'm still a guy and when given the challenge…

The chemo I was about to be subjected to had the potential of making me sterile. So the doctors wanted me to get some little Matthews put away before the treatment. I was guided into a little room of love by a smiling 40-something nurse. How nurses are able to keep straight faces through all the shit they have to do every day I have no idea. She left me to my own intimacies and I got down to business....

I was proud that I was able to "rise" to this particular challenge. I was also confused and scared in the event that I was unable to provide a sample. Being a little more understanding of my duty to carry on the family name, Dad had taken it upon himself to take me to the clinic on this day, and was waiting as I came out of the love room.

"How'd you go?" he asked optimistically and pretending not to know what I might have been doing for the last 10 minutes.

"I couldn't get anything..." was my reply.

I wasn't able to explain it very well as I didn't understand it myself. The nurse booked me in for another shot at the titles for the following day. I tried to tell Dad what had happened on the way home, this was no time to be hung up on modesty. I had been able to successfully masturbate without causing a tear in the surgical wound, but....how do I say this....as the whistle blew to charge, I found that none of my soldiers were leaving the trenches. There was no sperm. A medical term I was going to learn as "retrograde ejaculation". I must have been pretty unclear with my explanation. Dad contemplating the event came up with a great idea.

"Matt it's totally understandable that you are having trouble. There is nothing to be embarrassed about. If you like though, I can arrange for a "lady" to come along tomorrow and help you out."

Awesome, I now had Dad pimping for me! This was a first, and so I allowed myself a few moments to enjoy the proposal before better explaining the situation.

The following day brought a similar result. I had a meeting with Dr Sincere and I explained what was going on.

He explained to me what retrograde ejaculation was, and what was happening inside my plumbing area. There is a slight comfort you receive when a Doctor gives you a medical term and then explains an event that is happening in your body. It tells you that this stuff has happened before, that others have or are going through it and this makes you feel less alone, less scared of the unknown. The problem was however that the doctors were getting edgy. Time, remember, was not on my side. Just like the quote from the ageless military-bible movie Apocalypse Now – *Every day I was getting weaker, Charlie was getting stronger*. Even though we had removed the primary cancer source, the cancer had progressed into the advanced stages even before we had detected it. The insurgency had spread through my lymphatic system and I had a number of tumors sprouting their own destruction through my body. Every day we didn't start chemo was a loss of another 5-10 percent off my success rate (doctors seem to love those statistics).

We decided to try one more time to get a sample. This was more of a flanking manoeuvre that Dr Sincere came up with. We attempted to get a sample from my bladder. Again, something new here for me, but we were still in the New Year. I had to drink a solution before going into the love room to do my duty, and then went into the toilet where I produced a sample of urine. In some cases of retrograde ejaculation, the sperm can go into the bladder instead of coming out the business end. The magical medical people can then separate the sperm from the urine and come up with enough of a sample to freeze. Great idea hey? Unfortunately it didn't work. Why not? Well Dr Sincere was at a bit of a loss now. Our little flanking move didn't work and I was out of time. Do I look for a few other ways of getting a sperm sample and risk losing the whole war, or I do I give this piece of ground to the enemy and move on? Considering that I wasn't even married and didn't intend to be for a long time, I took a classic military move – a full frontal assault with lots of bullets and smoke … and chemicals.

"Bring on the chemo Doc!"

(During this awkward week, I had also been introduced to my oncologist). But to introduce him requires some background. Growing up in the country in Australia, and then becoming an Australian soldier had resulted in my succumbing to racism. I had grown a little untrusting of a number of races and cultures. I have no reason or justification for this attitude. As much pain and fear I was experiencing with this disease, I found myself in a dilemma when I discovered my oncologist was not "Caucasian". Cancer has taught me a great many lessons and I can honestly thank it for introducing me to this man and breaking me from a bad habit of being racially judgmental. Meeting Dr Not-Caucasian (Dr NC for short), was for me, a pivotal part of the war, as well as a turning point in how I viewed people.

Dr NC sat me down and went through the recipe. Putting it simply, chemotherapy is basically a combination of very serious, very toxic chemicals that are pumped into you. Oncologists will combine different solutions depending on what cancer they are fighting and come up with a recipe of poison that is then injected or administered by pills. Chemo is not good for you. In fact it kills you, but the plan is to get the chemo to kill the cancer before it kills you, and then you can recover from both. Make sense? Is the enemy of my enemy my friend? I had no idea, but Dr NC knew his shit and had rapidly won my trust. I knew I was being naïve, but this is how

I wanted to fight this at the moment:

"Doc you do what you have to do. Tell me what I have to do, and I'll do it."

The thought that I was going to have myself injected with poison just to piss off this cancer was kind of a nice feeling, a very Army feeling, and I was gaining some hope that we were moving forward again. Gaining the initiative, having forward momentum (offensive action) is a fundamental principle of warfare, and I was back on familiar ground. The three poisons we were going to hit this sucker with were: Cisplatin, Bleomycin and Etoposide. Bleomycin had the tendency to damage the lungs after prolonged exposure, so caution needed to be used to monitor my lung capacity and change the recipe at the right time.

"That's ok Doc. My lungs will put up with it. Should I quit smoking as well then?"

It might have been that I was reckless, going ahead without a sperm sample, not worrying about the side-effects of the chemo, still having the odd cigarette. But I was looking at this very simply – first I'll fight the cancer. Then I'll recover, and then I'll worry about the rest.

I was taken up to the chemo treatment room to meet the nurses, and some other cancer patients whom I would get to know over the following months. It struck me how (no offence guys), old the patients were. What did I have in common with them when I was 25 years old, in the Army and they were… older? Well we did have one obvious thing in common … we were all fighting cancer, fighting for our lives. The other thing that struck me about the room was the big recliner chairs. It seemed kind of strange at first but I soon realised that if you are going to sit down and get pumped full of toxic-cancer-killing-crap, then you might as well be comfortable when it's done to you. I made myself a little promise that WHEN I got through this cancer, I would invest in my very own recliner chair. (Note: as I finish this book I still have not come good with this promise to myself – but if I sell enough books…).

While we were getting to know the nurses, a very interesting conversation came up. One of the nurses mentioned that "she had heard" marijuana was reputed to ease the side-effects of the chemo. Of course professionally or legally she could not endorse nor confirm this. Mum was with me and was listening intently, nodding in concentration. She asked very seriously;

"And where could I get some of this marig-juana?"

I couldn't really believe my luck, in the last week, I had seen my dad offer to pimp for me, and now my mum was going to score some drugs for me! I suddenly had an understanding of what it might be like to have celebrity rock stars as parents … Being in the Army and probably somewhat of a martyr, I never did send Mum out on the streets to bring me some herbal relief, but looking back at it, and what chemo can put you through, I think I regret this.

Once the nurse and I had composed ourselves after Mum's comment, we made our farewells to everyone until the following day when things would get serious.

When people ask me what chemo is like I think the best analogy I have been able to come up with so far is this; "Imagine the worst hangover you have ever had. Then imagine it lasting for weeks and weeks and only getting worse. Then remind yourself that you didn't even get to have a good night out on the piss for your troubles."

So the chemo-campaign designed by Dr NC followed

this pattern:

> DAY 1 – massive chemo hit lasting a few hours. I would
> then be admitted into the hospital ward overnight so
> the nurses could monitor me and inject a huge amount
> of saline solution back into my system to re-hydrate and
> flush out the chemicals.
> DAY 2 – R&R (Rest and Recuperation).
> DAY 3, 4, 5 – Chemo hit (approx 1-2 hours).
> DAY 6 – R&R.
> DAY 7 – Chemo hit (approx 1-2 hours).
> DAY 8,9,10,11,12,13 – R&R.
> DAY 14 – Chemo hit (approx 1-2 hours).
> DAY 15,16,17,18,19,20 - R&R.
> DAY 21 – Start new cycle (Day 1).

In total I underwent six cycles of this treatment.

This was a three-week cycle. The first week was the all-out assault or surge. I was a walking chemical power plant, who by rights, should have glowed in the dark every time I pissed. This first week was so full on that I would then need about two weeks rest before I could do it again. We however, launched two follow-up assaults in those rest weeks, just to hold the initiative and keep the cancer off-balance. As I mentioned before, an oncologist is like a chief or an alchemist if you like - mixing the right recipe for each case of cancer. So chemo can be very different depending on the cancer you have and at what stage it is. I was never subjected to radiotherapy, which is useful when targeting a concentrated area where a cancer is. However, this chemo plan was still very intense. I was fortunate enough to have been given medical leave from the Army during this whole time. I don't know how I would have managed to work during this time if I hadn't had the luxury of great medical cover.

At the end of each cycle, I would get MRI scans, lung tests and blood tests. The lung tests were to ensure my lungs had not taken too much damage from the chemicals. Dr NC would then sit me down and go through the results. In regards to blood tests, or blood markers, I was tested on alphafeta protein and beta HCG. Before I started the chemo, my alphafeta protein blood markers were just under 15,000. These blood marker tests are a good general way of keeping track of the infiltration of cancer through the body. Anyone tested and getting under about 50 has no cause for concern. More than 250 and further tests are usually carried out as this number is classed as suspicious. In terms of testicular cancer, 7,000-8,000-plus is known as stage three (or advanced). My results from pre-chemo was the reason that Dr Sincere kept making me feel like a three-legged horse at Randwick (these results were gained from the web and are not exact, but you get the idea, right?)

Chemo is also degenerative. In this I mean that the first few times you get hit, you don't feel it that much, but the more times you are exposed to the chemicals, the worse you feel. My first cycle was not too bad. I remember a strange metallic taste in my mouth becoming slowly more obvious and a drain on energy. I also realised the wound from the operation to remove the teste wasn't healing. This was because my immune and regenerative systems were fighting now on three different fronts (fighting the cancer, fighting the chemo and trying to heal a wound). If you think back to World War II, Hitler was accused of losing that war by trying to fight on two fronts. The results upon conclusion of my first cycle were good – my blood markers were down to about 7,000. My cancer had just taken a 50 percent casualty hit from its first engagement with Dr NC's blitzkrieg of chemicals! This was as good a reason for celebration as I could remember for a while, so I had some of the boys from my old regiment take me out on the town.

I remember in those days being determined not to have cancer interfere with my social life. This resolution, along with a pretty stupid male ego saw me hitting the clubs a few times in those early cycles of chemo. I was also determined not to lose my sense of humour during the whole situation.

A mate of mine who was always up for some drinks (Morrie…) took me out to one of our locals called Shenanigans. He had some experience with cancer in his family and was talking about how well I was looking. The surprising thing was that as hairy a guy as I am, the chemo didn't seem to be affecting my hair growth. I agreed with him and reached up to grab a fist full of hair from my head. We both expected the hair to hold stubbornly on to the top of my scalp, but to both our amazement the whole clump came away from my head without any resistance. It turned us both a bit white as reality kicked in. Then we realised that we might be able to win a few drinks with this new party trick. My head soon started to look very unappealing and we decided this party trick was not going to help us with the girls. That weekend another friend of mine came to visit and ended up shaving my head bare, my hair was starting to clog up the pool filter. Welcome to the cancer club kiddo.

I was a smoker back then and decided that this was not the time to quit. My favorite response to that eternal; "I can't believe you are smoking with cancer!" comment was; "Well I already have cancer, what else can happen?" Anyway, I was on chemo, which one do you think is worse for my health?

When being confronted with a disease or situation that we feel we have no control over, we sometimes look for alternative destructive behaviour that we feel we can control. Smoking and drinking filled those roles for me.

Food fetishes are another side effect of chemo. I have heard these are similar to those felt by pregnant women. One night I was in my hospital bed and I received a call from Wal who was coming to visit me. He asked me if there was anything he could bring?

"Actually, some Macca's cheeseburgers would be great Mate."

"Are you serious? How many?"

"Just a few would be great."

He turned up with six! I ate five and he polished off the last one for me. I had never been a big McDonald's fan, and if anything I was a Big Mac kind of guy. I don't know what got into me that night but those cheeseburgers seemed to be the closest thing to heaven I had experienced in the last few weeks. The following cycle (three weeks later), Wal came to visit me in hospital again. He bought another five cheeseburgers. This time I wasn't feeling the same craving but thought I'd have a bite anyway. I made it through the first half before I had to run to the toilet and vomit it all up…

You know something is not good for you when the nurse puts on an outfit similar to a biological warfare suit before treating you. It never ceased to hit me with a pang of sadistic humour when I sat down in my recliner chair and the nurse put on thick industrial-plastic gloves and apron before handling the bag of radioactive solution that was just about to be injected into my veins.

The vomiting and nausea really started to hit me as I began the third cycle. I had been given an anti-nausea suppository (a rather large pill that does not go in through the mouth...), that could be taken daily. At first my pride and modesty limited the times I used it. Within a week, however, I had no hesitation in ducking off to the toilet and "throwing one up range" in search of some relief. These nausea waves would hit at any time. At home, at the movies, at the pub. I remember another night when a friend and I were at the pub and were going quite well with some young ladies. By now I was as bald as a badger and it was actually a bit of a talking point that we used as an "in" when trying to meet girls. I called it the sympathy-card line and it definitely was not going to go to waste. As we were there, however, I began to get some serious stomach cramps. I limped off to the toilet and experienced a horrid spate of diarrhea, including blood. No matter how much I tried to ignore it, I was sick, and my social life was going to be another casualty of this war.

I wasn't about to lie down and let chemo control my life though. When finally the wound healed from my first operation, I decided it was time to start getting fit again. I remember when I had first arrived in Darwin and I was in one of my initial consultations with Dr Sincere. He had been explaining cancer treatment and the chemo and as usual I was brushing most of the technical stuff aside.

"Now look, Doc, I am really into my training at the moment. Will any of this stuff stop me from going to the gym and exercising?" Well Mr Armstrong seemed to have been ok to do it (although I still had not started reading his book again since that day on the plane).

"Just take it easy and see how you feel." That impassive

face betrayed none of the ridiculousness of the question.

Yes I was riddled with cancer, and getting a large amount of chemo injected into me, but time still needs to be spent exercising the body and mind. There is a saying in the Defence Force; "You must fight to be fit, so you can be fit to fight."

I needed to make sure I was fit enough to continue the fight. The heat of the tropics and intensity of chemo, however, made it difficult to go running or weight training. Swimming became the focus of my training. I would go to Larrakeyah Army Barracks three times a week and swim as much as I could for an hour (it didn't matter if it was dog-paddling or free-styling, as long as I moved). No matter how sick I felt with chemo, I would go to that pool. I had to be careful as well with the sunlight as the chemo was making my skin hyper-sensitive. It didn't matter how sick I felt beforehand, once I had done my swim I found it helped. It definitely helped me to sleep when I got home – the type of sound, deep sleep you get from good physical training. Swimming became my focus as opposed to dreading the next chemo hit or going out and getting drunk (which was becoming an obvious and more irregular demon).

If I could offer one piece of advice to anyone going through a serious illness like cancer, I would suggest they find that one activity that they can do that provides some fitness, focus and direction. Swimming, walking, cycling – anything that keeps you moving in some way. Forward momentum is a key principle of offensive operations, and this training was another way for me to fight back at cancer.

I think it was around the end of my third cycle when Dr NC gave me a new twist to my situation. "Matthew, the chemotherapy is continuing to have a very good impact on the cancer. Your markers are continuing to decrease. But your immune system and lungs are now starting to degenerate significantly."

"Doc, do what you have to do. I'll worry about recovering." This was my standard response now.

"We will need to change the chemicals to try and not damage your lungs any further. Also, you will now need to give yourself an injection daily which will boost your immune system."

Great, now I am a diabetic as well. Being a big, tough bad-ass soldier meant that I was pretty much scared shitless of nothing – except needles. Now I was going to have to give myself one daily.

"I have arranged for a nurse to come around tomorrow and each day for the first week to give you the shot and teach you how to do it."

The nurse that came around the next day was an attractive young lady. I am not sure if Dr NC did this on purpose, but now I was forced to look tough and pretend that needles didn't bother me. Although I quite enjoyed having this nurse visit me daily, it took me three days before I told her that I was over the "sticking it to me" routine and that I was confident I could perform the task myself.

Things had seemed to reach a stalemate between the cancer and me. Chemo seemed to be the great leveler and that old saying kept running through my head whenever I sat down to have more of these toxins pumped into my veins; "The enemy of my enemy is my friend". At the same time as the needle was inserted into my arm, the wince of pain carried a little smile – "Hold tight little cancer I'm coming for you again." But how much of me was going to get destroyed in order to neutralise this insurgent? We had reached a stalemate and "we" (me and all my arrayed forces) had to just wait out and see which way the tide would turn. This was a classic war of attrition.

Two significant things happened during this time that would have resounding effects on my life, and ensured that I was reminded that the world continues to turn regardless of how much disease was inside me, or how much I tried to control it.

The first of these events was ANZAC day 2002. My first cousin was getting married in Newcastle and I had been invited along with the rest of the family. This was the first time I was really confronted with the fear of having a lot of people I knew see me in this diseased state. As superficial as it sounds, I had always been proud of my image as a soldier. I enjoyed the strong, proud and confident feeling that is derived from wearing a uniform and believing in a cause. When I was confronted with the decision of where to have my treatment, Darwin presented itself as the perfect safe base. Due to its distant location, I could also control how many people could visit me and when. I was in need of a place where I could be comfortable with the new and evolving image of myself as the cancer shaped me. As I am sure all cancer fighters will agree, this disease attacks your view of yourself. It, as well as the treatment, changes you physically, mentally, spiritually. You will never be the same person you were before you were diagnosed, and this is something that is very hard to come to terms with while people around you try to hang on to the person that "you" were before. So the thought of going back down South and seeing everyone from my old life was frightful. Was I ready for all the questions, side-looks, sympathy? I will admit that I was very close to declining and staying in Darwin until another offer was thrown up that took me by surprise. My stepfather Gordon and my dad served in the same Platoon in 9 RAR (long story for another book), and so it was proposed that if I went down for the wedding, then all three of us could march with 9 RAR in the Sydney ANZAC Day March. I am not sure where the logic was when I was ready to decline a family wedding because I was embarrassed about my physical and mental state, only to reconsider when the opportunity to march in front of thousands was offered while sickly and bald. Cancer or not, I was still a soldier and had a responsibility to show my respects on this day. I decided that this was a good idea, even if I was going to march with an Infantry Regiment (as opposed to a dashing Cavalry Regiment). I only hoped they would be able to keep in step with me!

We flew down to Sydney after getting a leave pass from Dr NC and the Army doctor who was managing my case. The chemo cycle and this trip seemed not to conflict, so providing I was able to be back in time for the following Monday's hit, I was fine to go. Apart from Mum's ever watchful eye, and the fact that she must have told every steward that I was to be treated extra-specially "because he has cancer", the flight was quite uneventful and I even began to read Lance's book again. We arrived at Sydney airport and hopped straight into a cab. The cab driver greeted me and asked me how I was, as if he knew me.

"Have you been swimming lately?" how did this guy know that I had been swimming up in Darwin?

"Yeah I have actually, but just taking it easy" – no point in lying.

"Are you still competing?" – Ok now this was a little

weird, Mum and Gordon in the back were just as confused.

"What do you mean?"

"You are Michael Klim aren't you?" – The penny dropped.

Being a bald bloke and having the slightest resemblance to the Olympic swimmer, I had got this Sydney Cabby all excited. I was pretty flattered with this mistake and it eased the tension I was feeling about coming down to Sydney. At least he hadn't mistaken me for someone with cancer...

That ANZAC day was a very weird experience. I recall sitting on the train on the way into the city, opposite a WWII veteran. He looked old and tired in his fading suit with a row of medals longer than his chest (and mine for that matter). I sat there looking at him, in my uniform, with no medals or hair, and feeling closer to death than him. I suddenly wondered if I should be wearing my uniform while I was in this state? Maybe I was no longer fit to wear it? Why was I doing this again? The march for me was hard. I was tired and nauseous from the chemo, my back was throbbing from simply standing around beforehand and I was not used to much physical exertion. The swimming at least gave me the chance to stop and catch my breath without the effects of gravity playing its part. But I was surrounded by people that had gone through war, real war, and were making this walk as well. This seemed to give me strength and my resolve was hardened by the experience of that day. In years to come I was going to realise that there is not that much of a difference between an internal war and an external one except, maybe, that with some external wars you are given the choice of whether to fight in it or not ... sometimes. Marching that day also helped me realise that no matter how sick I feel, or how much pain I am in, there are always people who have gone through, or are going through, worse. And when you survive, you survive for those who didn't as much as you survive for yourself. So a 25-year-old Cavalry Officer with testicular cancer marched in front of a regiment of veteran Infantrymen from the Vietnam War, with the banner being held by his two fathers AND we were all in step … for a little while.

After ANZAC day we headed up to Newcastle for the wedding. I was enjoying myself on this trip more than I had expected but I was still quite nervous about appearing in front of all my family and friends. It was during the reception that I met up with an old family friend whom you are going to know as The Angel-Whisperer. I am not going to go into too many details as to how I suddenly felt myself connecting with this young lady, or how surprised and flattered I was that she seemed to take an interest in me, but the relationship that was to follow, and continue for the next two years was going to have a big impact on how I started viewing life and death at a spiritual level. I had resigned myself to going through this battle more or less alone. I had my family, friends and a plethora of doctors. I did not have time for a "relationship", and I had been successfully dodging any serious commitment for quite some time and had no intention of letting my guard down now. Or so I thought. I tried to tell myself that I had no room in my head for love, but strangely enough, the more the cancer grew inside me, the more my heart desired that strange phenomenon that gives us more meaning in life.

Returning to Darwin I felt like I had been on R&R. I was refreshed, I had new resolve and a perspective on life and my situation, which was energising. Blood markers were continuing to go down and things were gaining momentum for the good guys. I was starting to see light at the end of this tunnel and caught myself wondering, "Life is good. What could go wrong?"

This is when the second event occurred that knocked me off balance. Todd, my best mate, who had visited me in Darwin and gone fishing with me just like we were 15 again, suddenly found himself in the middle of a terrifying war of his own. I was settling in to watch TV one night when the phone rang. "Hello."

"Yeah Matt, It's Todd here." His voice sounded formal, but he has always been one for the utmost politeness.

"G'day Mate, how's it going?" My mood was picking up as I was looking forward to having a good chin wag with him. "Umm, my brother's dead…" – the formality was still there but there was a shaking in his voice, which could no longer be controlled.

"You're kidding. What do you mean?" I have no idea why anyone would ring up and "kid" like that, and still cannot believe that I responded that way. I can only guess that I was so totally caught by surprise that I had no idea what I was saying.

Todd's brother had been killed in a car accident on his way home to see his parents. Now Todd had called me like I had called him, but so far I was not being very supportive. I asked him to explain what had happened. It amazed me how he was able to string sentences together and all I could do was listen. At the end of the call I told him I would call back in a few days when he had gotten himself back to Dubbo and spent some time with his family.

There are two reasons why this event affected me so much and why I decided to include it in this book. Firstly, I was instantly aware of my own inability to help my mate. I was not going to be able to drop everything and go back down South for him. I was tied down on my own front and by this stage the chemo was really starting to affect my health. I was simply just not well enough to travel. In the Australian Army in particular, mateship is extremely important and emphasised during training. When deployed on operations, and in the heat of deadly battle, the fear that is often felt by soldiers is not for their own safety, but for that of their mates. Mates will get you through an ordeal, or carry your body out and back home. Being a good mate is three-quarters of the way to being a good soldier. And here I was, unable to help .Todd understood this and never asked for me to come down, but it made me distinctly aware of my confinement, or in Army speak, I had lost my "freedom of action". Secondly, I realised just how close to death everyone is. It is not only those whose bodies are wracked with disease, or those in the middle of a war in Afghanistan or Iraq who sniff death in the wind. The healthy and happy can die just as quickly as the sick, the brave or the old. Furthermore, I realised how lucky I was to be given a chance to put up a fight! Sometimes we don't get to say "good-bye", and sometimes those days that we feel the sickest, are the days when we can actually feel the most alive. Survival for me was no longer going to be just a matter of war-gaming for the future and dreaming about what I was going to do when I got "better"; it needed to be about acknowledging and making the most of the present. I started to feel very mortal, and this feeling had its own liberation.

The chemo campaign was drawing to an end. I sat in the office of Dr NC as he briefed me on the latest intelligence report from the frontline. My blood levels were now at the stage where I "technically" no longer had cancer! Could I be so bold to call myself "cured"? Call me a pessimist, or just a realist, but I did not feel waves of relief crash over me. There was no primal roar of victory. It didn't feel like this was the end yet. I felt like I had won a battle, but not the war. And I was pretty much on the money. First, the doc wanted me to go through one more cycle of chemo. This was as a good measure hit to make sure we had totally smashed all cancerous elements in my body. This was something I really didn't feel like doing as I already had quite enough toxic, radioactive crap pumped into me, but he was the Doc. My only job was to put up with it. Mum and Gordon took me to a pub along Darwin's waterfront to celebrate our good news. I think mum needed to see this as a win more than I. I started to realise how much of a strain my illness was putting on her, and the rest of my family. My drinking had reduced quite significantly over the last few months or so but I still indulged in a glass of champagne. Mum was really excited and it was hard to put a curb on her optimism. I asked her nevertheless to hold the big celebrations as we were not out of the woods yet. Mum politely told me to let her enjoy this moment and I would do well to enjoy it as well … I gave in and allowed myself to relax.

After what seemed like an eternity, but was actually three weeks, I completed my final cycle of chemo and came back down south for another break. By now I was officially dating The Angel-Whisperer, and we were going to spend some time in the Hunter Valley wine region before I started what was to be called "the mop-up campaign", (surgery to remove any remaining tumors). While I was on this break I was introduced to a friend of the Angel-Whisperer classed as a spiritual healer. I had never really heard of this type of thing, and what I did know of it I didn't really believe. But, as the name would hint,

The Angel-Whisperer was very much into this stuff and had been slowly preparing me for what was to come. Of the many things that cancer has taught me, having an open mind is up there as one of the most important things I have learnt. (And patience). Although I did not agree, believe or understand alternative methods of healing, I figured "what doesn't kill me, can only make me stronger". So I went along to this session with no idea what I was in for…

I sat on a seat in the middle of a smallish room. The healing centre had been converted from a house and the consulting rooms were the old bedrooms. The "healer" was sitting opposite me, another lady was positioned behind the seat I had been directed towards, and Ms Angel-Whisperer had decided to join the session and was sitting off to the left. All three ladies sat very upright with the palms of their hands facing up, resting on their laps. The healer asked me to sit down and try to relax. This wasn't easy as I felt like I was caught in a fucking ambush. I had one person on my 6 o'clock, one at my 9 o'clock and one engaging me from the front – relax? like hell!

"How are you feeling Matthew?" I was either in trouble or she was being very formal. Only Mum called me Matthew, and usually when I was in strife.

"Pretty good" (besides having cancer, being bald as a badger and missing a nut, how did she think I was feeling?)… Was my cynicism showing? Could she read my mind? Fuck. This was weird.

"How have you been emotionally during this experience?" The Healer maintained a very calm, nurturing voice.

"Pretty good. I have been able to keep my emotions pretty well under control during this whole event". I wasn't about to start lying to her and this was a fact that I had been quite proud of.

The Healer lost a bit of her composure as she stifled something between a laugh and a snort of disgust.

"Matthew, emotions are there to be experienced and expressed, not controlled or ignored". She explained this sagely. I frowned in disagreement. Not where I'm from sister, I thought, but kept this to myself.

"Now I need you to relax and let your energy flow, we are going to clean out your aura."

This all sounded very magical and lovely. I had no real idea what she was talking about, but to my credit I tried to relax.

"Matthew, your 'chakras' are all closed, you have to relax."

"Um … ok, sorry." What the fuck is a chakra? Anyone? And why do I feel like I am in trouble?

I sort of lost time in there and eventually the healing session finished. I didn't feel any different, but I was assured that some good work had been done and that my energy was flowing a bit better. The healer was impressed and I felt confused, but strangely proud of myself.

This moment marked the beginning of a spiritual search that has still not ceased, but has given me strength and consolation when I am forced to ask questions that have no answers. Although I felt absolutely nothing during that energetic healing session, and have had a lot of similar experiences with many other alternative health methodologies since, I did realise that I needed some form of discipline to focus my resolve around. For all their differences, energetic and alternative health methods all seem to have one thing in common. They promise to empower you. At the same time though, you have to be careful that you do not become a sheep following some mystical sensation. There can only be one general in charge of an army. These practices allow you to take control of your life in some small way and allow you to help yourself.

The power of the mind is amazing and is something we still have very little knowledge of. Whereas with western medicine the patient seems to be totally reliant on the doctor to heal or cure them, these alternative methods can empower the sufferer by helping them believe that there is more they can do themselves. I would totally encourage anyone going through cancer, or any ordeal, physical or mental, to try out these alternate health practices. You just might find something that connects with you and if nothing else, gives you some meaning for what is going on … providing some faith to hold onto. But be careful and mindful of what is out there. Believe nothing that advocates a quick and easy cure to your disease. Unfortunately you are in for a fight either way you look at it and this fight will take time. I was to find a method that connected with me more powerfully further down the track, but for the time being, this soldier was not going to go dancing with the fairies.

I am not sure if the chemo had shrunk the massive tumor in my abdomen that was causing the back pains, or if the chemo had made me so sick that I had just forgotten the pain. But it was while I was in the Hunter Valley that I started getting vicious pains again, and fear took over where the cancer had left off. I quickly rang back to Darwin for advice. I feared that the cancer was back already. The chemo had failed, and things were going to get bad again. Dr NC returned my call and calmed me down. Although he was concerned by what was going on, he was confident that the chemo had neutralised the cancer and I did not need to worry. We were on a wine tour at the time of this conversation and I was getting some very impatient looks from the other tourists eager to get to the next vineyard. The Angel-Whisperer was trying to settle them down and explain that I was on the phone to a doctor. These people and their wine tasting were the last things on my mind, but then again, I guess some random guy with cancer issues was the last thing on their minds – bring on the wine!

Dr NC explained that although the chemo had been effective against the cancer, the residual mass of the tumor was still there. It was now most probably benign instead of malignant. The problem was that this tumor mass still had the ability to grow, even though it was benign. It seemed that my cancer was very aggressive and so too was the tumor mass left behind. I couldn't help but be a little impressed. This really was my disease, and it wasn't going to give up without a fight. R&R was over boys. Time to get back in this war…

Now that the chemo had done its job and the "cancer" had been neutralised, Dr NC took a back seat. He would continue to monitor my progress and blood results, but now it was time to get Dr Sincere back into the fight. If chemotherapy is your conventional force that adopts the classical "attrition" approach to warfare, then surgery is more like your "special operations". It consists of precise, well-planned and delicate surgical procedures that are aimed at taking out very specific threats that are located next to or within vital organs of the body. Dr Sincere ordered a number of scans and tests and effectively conducted a reconnaissance of my body to detect what and where these threats were. He found a fair bit.

Although my body had responded well to the chemo, and had stopped the cancer as effectively as a 50 caliber machine does advancing infantry, the cancer was so advanced by this time that it had established its own Forward Operating Bases (the tumors), throughout my body, primarily within lymph nodes. Some cancers tend to follow the lymphatic system as they advance through the body, and mine had set up bases in my abdomen, chest, lungs and neck. Where do we start?

The tumor sticking out of the left side of the base of my neck was at the top of the list. It was relatively easy to remove compared to the others and it would give the scientists an opportunity to analyse it (conduct a biopsy) and see what we were dealing with. Sounded very military to me and I liked it!

I liked the thought of these operations, more so than the chemo. How hard can operations be? They put you to sleep, do the work, and then wake you up. All you have to do then is heal and recover … easy. The neck operation went extremely well. My body was still recovering from the effects of the chemo, but the immune and regenerative systems were starting to kick back in and my recovery rate was exceptional. It was so good in fact that I was feeling on top of the world the day after the operation. Dad had arrived from the Gold Coast to spend some time with me and came into my hospital room around mid-morning.

"How you feeling Mate?" Dad's ocker greeting was always welcome.

"Yeah, really good, I could even go for a beer!" I wasn't even putting this on. I felt really good.

"Well do you want to go for one? I'll take you out for lunch?" The offer sounded just as good and I accepted without thinking.

I got dressed and we left the room. Passing the nurses desk I told the girl on duty that I was just popping out with Dad. She was pretty busy and waved at me. All the nurses in Darwin Private knew me pretty well by this stage. (I had even asked one out on a date during chemo – no luck), and she didn't seem too concerned. Dad took me to a pub and I had a pint of Guinness and a steak. I love my food and the chance to get a good meal into me as opposed to hospital food was graciously accepted. The neck was a little tender, it was dressed well and I thought the sunlight was good for me.

We returned to the ward around two-and-a-half hours later and walked straight into frontal fire. It seems that I was not allowed to leave the hospital without being signed out by a doctor, and after the operation, this was not to occur for another few days. Definitely no pub outings the day after! The nurse we had spoken to thought we meant we were going outside for some fresh air or a smoke, not lunch. I felt terrible as this poor lass had been torn apart by the doctor when he came around to do his rounds, and no one had any idea where we were. If I felt bad, Dad was visibly limping. The hospital had rung Mum at home and she was there waiting too. She took Dad aside and I think if they had not already been divorced, this would have been the result of that day's events.

The results from the biopsy came back extremely positive, the tumor was a benign teratoma. Basically residual mass left over from the cancer. If there was still cancer in my body, it would be lurking in these tumors and we all relaxed with these results. But this was the easiest of the operations. I sat down with Dr Sincere to war-game our next surgical strike. I had a multitude of tumors in both lungs, but individually they were all quite small. The main threat came from the large mass in my abdomen. Although Dr Sincere was sure we needed to go straight after this tumour, the size and magnitude of the tumour meant the operation would be massive, he had never actually performed an operation of this size before and needed to do serious research before "going in". I was confident of his ability and told him so. He hadn't let me down yet, and he was an integral Captain in my Army. Still the hesitation in his eyes remained.

Prior to performing the operation, a bed in the intensive care unit (ICU) had to be available for when I came out of the operation. It was expected that I would be in there for a few days under observation before being released into the general ward. A bed was expected to be free in the next week, so the day was locked in and everyone began their battle preparations for the upcoming assault. I had little to do in the form of preparation but I ensured my swimming program was maintained. On the eve of the operation I was given a very big dose of medicinal laxatives to clean out my bowels. This was my first ever abdominal operation and I had never taken one of these before. I was warned that once I took this medicine I was to stay home and not be too far from the toilet. That was some of the best advice I have ever had. This stuff ripped through me like a mounted charge through unsuspecting foot infantry! No sooner had I sat back down from going to the toilet, I was back up again with the next round of stomach cramps. Within two hours I was exhausted, very dehydrated and kind of felt like I had already "discarded" any large mass in my belly. Mum woke me up the next morning and I hopped out of bed feeling considerably lighter. I was administered and the nurses began the pre-op procedures. The vibe was pretty good and I was relatively relaxed. Dr Sincere arrived about an hour after I was supposed to be collected. By the look on his face he was about to be renamed Dr Frustrated. It turns out the bed in ICU was not available and the operation had to be cancelled. Crap. Failure to launch. We were told to go home and he would call when another date could be arranged.

A week later and we were ready for the second attempt. I was going through that god-awful procedure of "clean-out" and I remember thinking that at least my chances of bowel cancer would be significantly reduced after all this. About 10 o'clock that night we got another phone call from Dr Sincere – now openly frustrated. There had been a bad car accident and the ICU was full again – stand down soldier.

This caused some obvious distress to all of us and we sat down with the doctor the following day. He said that he could not assure me that this would not happen again. He continued on by suggesting that I should reconsider the option to go down to Sydney for this operation.

"Doc, I get the feeling you don't particularly want to do this operation?" This time the seriousness was from my side.

"Matthew, I will do the operation if you want me to, but I think you should go to Sydney where the facilities and support are better." If I respected this guy before, I loved him now. He couldn't be more honest about what he was, and was not, going to be able to provide for me.

Looking back now, all the signs pointed me towards Sydney. If I believed that there was someone upstairs looking out for me, then I think they were definitely making their intentions known. Darwin had served its purpose, but this next part of the fight was going to require some bigger guns.

"Well then, let's go south."

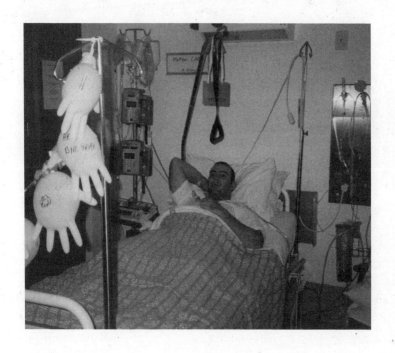

# SYDNEY

*"When your quarry goes to ground, give them no ground to go to."*

*Dear Dr Rather-Be-Fishing,*

*Thanks for asking me to see Matthew Carr, a 25 year-old man with a recently diagnosed right testicular cancer. As you know, this was initially diagnosed earlier this year after a presentation of lower abdominal pain. He was found to have widespread disease with a retroperitoneal mass, lung mestases, and a left supraclavicular fossa mass. He had a markedly alpha-fetroprotein following his left orcidectomy, although I do not currently have the complete history of his treatment in Darwin.*

*He went on to have treatment with Bleomycin, Etoposide and Cisplatin chemotherapy and received a total of six cycles. However, his Bleomycin was suspended after eight doses because of pulmonary problems. Once again, I don't know the speed with which his markers fell but I understand it may have been a little slower than one would have hoped. He completed his chemotherapy in early July and has been well since that time. He did, however, have a residual mass in his left supraclavicular fossa and this has been resected with histological finding being mature teratoma.*

*He has been sent down to Sydney for consideration of resection of his residual abdominal mass. However, in reviewing his CT scans, I am a little concerned that his most recent CT scans from the 13th August may in fact show some progression of his pulmonary metastases.*

*Physical examination today is relatively unremarkable. He has an easily palpable abdominal mass but with little else to find. He does have some reduction in sensation in his finger tips in keeping with the paraethesia he has been experiencing since the conclusion of his chemotherapy.*

*Before deciding how best to treat Matthew, I think we need to try and establish whether he has active malignancy at present. I have repeated his alpha-fetoprotein and beta HCG today and will be having his scans reviewed.*

*If there is a suggestion that his tumour is still active, I really think we should be getting on with salvage chemotherapy, probably complimented by high dose chemotherapy with otologist stem cell support. On the other hand, if his markers are normal, it might be worth trying to get a PET scan before any surgery again just to be certain that he doesn't have active malignancy. I will try and talk to you directly to discuss this and will let you know what happens once I have gotten further information from the Northern Territory.*

*Kind Regards,*
*Doc Rabbit.*

I arrived in Sydney and was met by the Angel-Whisperer. Neutral Bay was going to be my initial HQ at least until after the operation. From there the preparations for the upcoming operation began. I had a number of new medical staff recruited and waiting to be briefed and they were going to ask a lot of questions. My new oncologist – Doc Rabbit, at times seemed even more serious than Dr Sincere, but then he would change and be quite relaxed. He also hopped around his offices quite quickly – a very hard man to keep up with if you were following him to his consulting room or to the chemo rooms. His rabbit-like energy was also portrayed in his work ethic – he was a very busy, very qualified and a very likable man. Still, it was going to take me some time to warm to him (or maybe him to me), perhaps because I was starting to run low on the energy required to continually meet new specialists who I knew were going to put me through some other form of painful treatment. He had very little to do with me at this stage as the cancer had all but vanished, and he would just monitor from the flanks unless a resurgence occurred. I remember being pretty adamant that this guy and I were not going to get to know each other to the same extent as Dr NC. I was referred onto a urological surgeon for the operation on the mass in my abdomen. As much as I didn't enjoy the fact that I was continually meeting all these new doctors, each with their own specialty in cutting me up or poisoning me, I will admit that it has been my good fortune to meet some truly extraordinary people whom I would never have come across had I had not been diagnosed. Dr Rather-Be-Fishing is one of these people.

This man had a manner of speaking that I appreciated, very honest and matter-of-fact, yet with a slight grin on his face that made me wonder if he was actually imagining himself hooking onto a massive Barramundi as opposed to confronting people with life-threatening disease each day.

"Now Matthew you're a very complicated case..." – I wasn't sure if he was talking about me or my condition.

"...It's going to be a really big operation, and it's going to hurt..." – Doc, after chemo I'm thinking this will be a walk in the park.

"...there maybe be other complications that arise from the operation. Quadriplegia, kidney damage and death are all possibilities." – Yes that could complicate things, especially if I had aspirations of leaving the Army and ever getting a real job that required me to be ... alive.

One very useful trait that I developed in the Army was the ability to remain "mission focused". A war is usually a long and complicated conflict that involves numerous battles and requires one side to achieve a number of objectives to gain some form of dominance or advantage over the other side (the obvious advantage being that the enemy is all dead and you are not). Unless you are Alexander the Great, looking at a whole war and wondering how you are going to win it can be very depressing. Instead, it is better to break it down into smaller pieces or "objectives" and then deal with each battle individually. Therefore each battle will have a "mission" that must be achieved in order meet the objective. To me, being mission focused meant that I needed to just worry about each operation at a time. If complications did occur, then I would deal with them as they arose.

"Doc, you just do your bit, and I'll handle the recovery" – and of course, a soldier always needs to be optimistic, because the alternative is pretty shit.

Even after the two operations in Darwin, I was still looking at a minimum of four more procedures; one abdominal, two for the lungs and one more in the neck (a bit of tumor had remained from the first neck operation and had now grown back), and my back hair had not yet even returned since the chemo! Mission-focused and stubbornly optimistic would do me just fine.

I think it was becoming obvious to The Angel-Whisperer that I was not totally embracing the divine mother within my soul. Considering my past experiences with martial arts, she tried a different tact and introduced me to a Chinese Qigong Master (pronounced *Chi Kung*), named Zhao. Qigong is relatively unknown in the Western world but is massive throughout Asia and especially China. It has many different aspects (health, spirituality, combat conditioning, and longevity) and is the reason why those freaky little Shaolin Monks can be suspended 10 foot in the air by a spear in their belly and not be impaled. In basic terms, Qigong can be described as a mix between Tai Chi and Yoga. It usually involves some really weird exercises that appear intent on making the practitioner look as ridiculous as possible, but end up making you feel really good (for a better explanation you might want to Google it). Zhao had been learning this art since he was three years old and has achieved great results with people suffering from chronic fatigue syndrome, cancer and a whole bag of ailments, conditions and diseases. I'm not sure if it was due to Zhao's infectious personality or the fact that I understood the exercises and philosophy after years of martial arts training, but this form of alternative treatment hit a deep chord within me. I had finally found something "spiritual" that I could actually grab onto. Qigong had no religious affiliation or bias, I didn't have to ask permission from angels or the divine mother for forgiveness or help, and most of the exercises were physical and practical. Yep, this was more like a soldier's medicine.

Within the space of a few weeks I had met my newly recruited forces, both medical and spiritual, grown some new eyebrows, and was again taking that awesome diuretic that would remove any food elements that I may have ingested since Darwin.

A soldier's bravado and practical philosophy aside, the night before this operation would have to be, up until that moment, the scariest time of my life. The feeling can be easily related to that of a soldier preparing to go into a real shooting match. I was finally beginning to grasp the brevity of my situation. Reflecting on this feeling since, I believe that realising I had absolutely no control over what was about to occur to me was the most confronting. In war it seems easier. At least there you have a rifle, your mates around you, fitness, aggression, and…consciousness. Instead, I was about to walk into a hospital, let these people put me to sleep and then what? Would I wake up? Would I still be able to walk? Would the tumour be gone? This wasn't going to be as simple as I had let myself think. I was not the only person feeling anxious that night. The family had rallied around me and it was obvious by the strained, shallow conversations that everyone was experiencing the same unease. We had arranged to have dinner at my relatives in Newtown. This was a punishing night because my uncle (who is quite the cook), was serving up his special homemade pizzas. Great for all those eating! Due to my pre-op preparations and the process of weeing out of my bum every 15-20 minutes, I wasn't able to eat anything. It was a very surreal night where everybody talked, laughed and discussed everything that could be considered normal conversation, and we all tried to avoid the upcoming engagement.

Before going to sleep I tried to write a will. I felt that even though I was determined to wake up, I should still have a backup plan. I needed to write something down just in case. This was actually easier said than done. What the hell do I write?

"Cheers Mum – thanks for all those chicken mornays!"

"Cheers Dad – I'd give you a hug but we're blokes, and blokes don't do that shit."

"Cheers Sis – you can have my Holden Ute if you want it. (Top set of wheels, but there is a bit still owing on it".)

"Make sure you burn the ashes and spread them on the wings of a wedge-tail eagle. I thought of this once when I was 16 and experimenting with pot and thought it was the coolest idea I had ever had."

"You guys can fight over the $618 in my savings account.

Minus the cost of catching the eagle. Ask the Army to cover the funeral costs."

My massive manuscript of a will, apparently my final wise and loving comments to a world I was going to leave behind on my journey across the river Styx, ended up being one-and-a-half scribbled A4 pages using a Bic pen. And not really saying anything at all...

"Fuck it I'll just make sure to wake up instead," and with that I went to sleep at 2-ish.

0600 hours - The alarm goes off with an angry, piercing tone that drags me out of a dreamless sleep with all the subtlety of my Drill Sergeant at Duntroon. I roll out of bed with as much enthusiasm as I did back then. Throw on my uniform, strap up my boots. Grab my helmet. Webbing and rifle are collected last as I stride purposely out the door. We step off the line at 0900, but I have to be at the staging area well before that for battle prep and orders. No hot brew this morning to warm the nerves and fingers – the smell might give away our position to the enemy close by. There is just the crisp air-conditioned coolness of a very big, white and sterile hospital to sharpen the senses. With all my years of training and all those day-time dreams of being in the midst of a raging battle, I never thought I would go into my own personal war wearing a gown that had a split right down the back and my arse hanging out. Although talk to any of my mates that I have served with and they'll claim that I always had my arse hanging out due to disorganization, regardless of the uniform.

When I woke up from the operation everything was a bit hazy. I knew where I was, and I remember asking how it all went. The family was around and I was told that the operation went well. My left arm wasn't responding, why isn't my arm working? I had tubes hanging out everywhere. It looked strange and felt even stranger. In fact I couldn't feel anything at all. Fuck my mouth is dry. Then I passed out again. I spent about a week in ICU and then a few more days in the high-dependency ward. Of that I remember some very weird dreams involving a gang of very loud and annoying pigeons, and owning a winery that went bust and thinking how funny it was that I would be walking away from the wine industry with exactly the same as what I had when I came into it - nothing.

Although I was in a lot of pain, I don't really remember being in pain until I was moved into the normal ward. I also remember Mr Woo. He and I were total strangers, but we spent the last few days of his life next to one another. I can clearly remember the couple of times this stranger's electronic monitors beeped and blared and the nurses calling out his name in an attempt to wake him, pleading for him to keep breathing. I remember because when they started calling out, so did I. For some reason it felt like we were allies egging each other across no-man's land (or was that all a dream as well?). Mr Woo died, I think. It made me feel sad even though I had no idea of the situation I was in. Another fallen comrade – "Don't worry Mr Woo, I'll get get those bastards for you". The ICU I was in is different to how I saw it through the drugs. All that is left of a whole week of my life is wrapped up in a few chaotic hazy memories – Mr Woo, my special friend Michelle, and one of her sisters visiting me and me getting a kiss from both of them and me commenting that even in this poor state I was able to get kisses from pretty girls, the high dependency ward seemingly being located in a pleasant little French provincial country club laced with creeping ivy.

The operation was conducted at the Royal Prince Alfred. At that time, the hospital was very under-staffed. ICU requires a nurse for each patient. Once in the general ward, however, the ratio of nurse to patients blows out considerably. It was easier for my family to take turns in sitting by my side almost 24 hours a day so that I didn't have to wait two hours to be cleaned up after vomiting. I wasn't moving too quickly during those days and I was also chained to the bed by tubes and drips so making it to the toilet was usually unachievable. The nurses that were there were great and another chauvinistic barrier of mine broke when I needed the help of a gay nurse to shower all my parts each morning. His sense of humour and my incapacity to help myself combined to overcome any homophobic attitude I may have had in the past. I had my 25th birthday in the general ward of the RPA. The nurses blew up surgical gloves and tied them to a cord and strung them up across my bed like balloons. A cake was brought in and friends, family, staff and fellow sicklies all had cake, except for me who had been on "nil by mouth" for two or three weeks. I was allowed the treat of having some small cubes of ice placed in my mouth. As everyone does on their birthday, I over indulged and ended up vomiting all that ice up an hour or so later. Life was never meant to be too easy I guess.

Once I was in the general ward, my main focus was to fart. For the first time in my life, everyone wanted me to drop my guts! But the trick was not to pop any staples in the process and literally drop my guts. The passing of wind would indicate to the doctors that my bowls, intestines and all the other parts were settling down after being removed from my belly cavity, placed on a table, cut/snipped/sifted, and then returned. It was kind of like test-firing your automatic rifle after disassembling it, cleaning it and then going through the reassembly. While waiting for the magical moment of flatulence I was able to while away the hours by standing for limited time, and counting out the five-minute intervals between self-induced morphine hits.

One day I was taken down to the imaging centre for some x-rays to monitor how everything was going. I had been getting some bad stomach cramps which was a sign that things were on the move. Again, the staff was quite busy and overrun and after the scan, I was left in the hall-way for "someone" to wheel my bed back up to the ward. I had been there for about an hour and the cramps increased in severity, I knew that I needed to go to the toilet but I was unable to get myself out of the bed due to all the drains and cords, not to mention the fact that I wasn't really strong enough to walk on my own, even if I had known where the nearest toilet was. The last of my pride left me that day at the same time as bodily fluid came out my rear end for the first time in three weeks, in a trolley bed, in the imaging centre hallway at RPA. If nothing else in my body was working, at least I knew my nose was. Since my diagnosis with cancer, friends and family alike have commented on the various changes in me; an increase in patience and humility being two of the more significant changes. Although these are both changes I am proud of, I rarely explain that a big part of the lesson involved lying in my own diarrhoea for 45 minutes. A soldier's optimism will tell you that at least it was not 48 minutes before I was wheeled back to my room, and a shower. Dr Rather-be-Fishing was excited to hear of the bowel movement although I was not really sharing in his delirium. This moment was in fact a turning point in my recovery. My progress increased dramatically as drains were able to be removed. However, I insisted on pulling out the catheter myself – not an enjoyable feeling, and I was soon mobile and going outside for breaths of fresh air. A good definition of irony that I would like to see included in the dictionary – *hospital patients (sick people), who go outside for a breath of fresh air and light up a cigarette.* (Can you guess who the reformed smoker is?)

Of all the most uncomfortable and painful moments of my time in that hospital during that particular operation, there was one incident that stood out the most. If I have failed to mention enough times already, I am a man of significant hair growth (wookie, silver-back and yeti are but a few nicknames I have been labelled with over the years). The chemo had temporarily turned me into very large pre-pubescent, silky-smooth lad, but since I had ceased the treatment several weeks prior, the hair was beginning to return. There was little hair when I was first operated on, but during my recovery there was further growth (remember that a lot can happen with the body in three weeks). One day one of the nurses came in wanting to change the dressing that was covering the surgical staples holding my guts together. These went from the bottom of my sternum all that way down to my navel, with a perpendicular cut from above my belly button out to the right stopping on the side of my torso, like a capital "T" lying on its side. The dressing was medical "sticky tape" and it was stuck to my skin, my wound and the staples, and now the newly grown body hair. My nurse was sweating with concentration and sympathy. Within seconds, I had my finger permanently pressed on the morphine button and my eyes clamped shut. I have thankfully never been subjected to torture in a POW camp, but this event would definitely be on any terrorist "let's try" list. It was kind of like getting a slow wax job over an open wound.

The day of my release from hospital saw me self-showered, self-dressed and waiting impatiently for the Angel-Whisperer to pick me up. The patience I was bragging about earlier on was still in its fledgling stage. I walked painfully to the car, was driven home, and got myself up the stairs and onto the couch where I fell asleep instantly due to exhaustion. After a 15-hour operation to remove a 3 kilogram tumor, four weeks in hospital (three of those without food), a kidney no longer functioning due to surgical complications, and permanent nerve damage to my left arm, I guess I could wait until tomorrow before starting the whole rehab thing. I can still hear my mind-voice explaining that I would never have to go through something like that again ... all good intentions aside – never say never. Blissfully ignorant, I had about seven years to get as healthy and fit as possible before jumping back into a fire-fight like that again.

The apartment where I was staying was located on Young Street in Cremorne. It had a small rectangular park behind it, measuring 50 by 200 metres, stretching up a small hill with a 20-degree slope. This pleasant little park would be the training ground for my initial rehab. What surprised me was that after such a massive operation, I was released from hospital with no rehabilitation or dietary plan. I do not know if I was supposed to ask or if it was not considered but it was an issue that I decided to take into my own hands. The first stage was to start walking again, and so at 0830, a week after my release, I was standing at the bottom of that slight inclining slope. It took me about 10 days before I was able to make it to the top in one go where there was a conveniently placed park bench. Within a few weeks, however, I was up and down that hill like a sprightly 90-year-old. Things were picking up.

I had roughly five months before going back in for the lung operations so I needed to use this time productively and build up my strength as much as possible. The Angel-Whisperer and I moved into a house in Riverview. Cremorne had been a great location, but the apartment we were in was small, and I had to make room for a very special companion. This rental allowed pets in the backyard and so I was quick to fly Hector down from Darwin to help me with my morning walks.

It is not uncommon for soldiers who have experienced combat to suffer from "battle stress". This occurs when an individual has been exposed to the trauma of combat for too long or the intensity of the combat was so great that the mind, and body, stresses out and begins to shut down. Reactions to battle stress vary from individual to individual. In the past soldiers suffering from it were seen as cowards and it was only in the late twentieth century that militaries realised battle stress was a valid medical condition and something to be factored into training. At Duntroon, we undergo a sleep and food deprivation exercise to experience battle stress in a simulated and controlled environment. One of the purposes is for cadets to understand the effects. Looking back at those months of recovery after the operation, I can plainly see that I was experiencing battle stress, the most obvious sign being that I can remember very little of that time. I know that I walked Hector daily and became somewhat shy of social interaction. The days, however, just seemed to have just passed on by with no real distinction or memory.

A very military method of working through battle stress is to keep busy. Soldiers with no direction and nothing to do are very dangerous, to themselves and to people around them, and this can have an adverse effect on morale. In this haze I remember that I slowly began to make decisions to regain some forward momentum. A mate of mine lent me a wind-trainer for my bicycle and as well as my daily walks with Hector, I began doing some stationary cycling. I began cooking – something that I had never really been into. I took control of my diet and soon became very conscious of the food that I ate. I also went back to Zhao for Qigong treatment and meditations. This gave me the spiritual strength I needed to comprehend what I had gone through.

Christmas 2002 came and went, and I headed up to Dad's in Tweed Heads for New Year's Eve. Tweed Heads/ Coolangatta is quite unique on New Year's Eve as the locals are treated to two celebrations to welcome the New Year. Because of daylight saving and the time difference between NSW and QLD, locals line up along the foreshore at Tweed to watch the midnight fireworks, have a drink and line up for a kiss with whomever they are standing next to. Then everyone saunters over the road and does it again in Coolangatta! It is very festive and very crowded. That year as our little squad negotiated the crowds, I suddenly felt very vulnerable and weak. I was not enjoying myself and was keen to go home but was trying to fight through this at least until the fireworks were over. Fireworks are pretty much air-burst artillery shells filled with coloured gun-powder. I love them and always hear Wagner's *Ride of the Valkeries* in my head as a barrage of light assaults a night's sky. This evening, however, turned suddenly very symbolic and memorable as I realised that I almost didn't see the beginning of 2003. Again, I started to cry as I realised just how close I had come to death. Symbolic, as it wasn't artillery or gunshot that had almost taken me, but a silent, elusive disease that was in me. Part of me.

I returned to Sydney and began preparations for the next offensive. Although I was still far from recovered from the last operation and the hair was only just starting to grow on my back again, the doctors were keen to press the advantage. I was introduced to a cardiovascular surgeon named Dr Chocolate-Love. This charismatic but daunting figure is absolutely obsessed with chocolate. He explained the upcoming procedure in which he would be going into my lungs from my back, working between the ribs. He would deflate one lung and work at "clipping" out the small tumors that had been spotted in the scans. These spots were numerous and in both lungs. Unfortunately this meant that both lungs would have to be operated on. Considering that it is not feasible to operate on both lungs in one hit, I would be undergoing two separate operations. Dr Chocolate-Love must have seen the concern in my eyes and continued by explaining that "all going well", my recovery from each operation should be quite quick. So quick in fact that there would only be one week separating the two operations!

This was tough for me to comprehend. I liked the thought of smashing through these operations quickly, but with the memory of the last operation still very fresh in my mind (and the scar still very pink on my body), I was doubtful about of the speed of recovery being explained by the surgeon. Of course I had the option to spread these out further but decisive and aggressive action often keeps the enemy off balance. This is how I had been trained and I saw no reason to doubt this mind-set now. Dr Chocolate-Love's confidence and aggressive attitude towards the tumours encouraged me to take his advice.

I was horrified to realise how accustomed I was becoming to relatively large operations. I was much more confident and reckless with my body than I am now, but this approach did what needed to be done at the time. Similar to a soldier getting up each morning and returning to the front line or heading out on another day's patrol with the knowledge that contact with the enemy was imminent, I would almost march into the hospital with a gait that telegraphed a mixture of alertness and aggression, but at the same time with the wariness of a battle-fatigued veteran. I have noticed that with each operation, adrenaline more than fear is the dominating force. This is how I fight and surgery would be seen as nothing different.

The lung operations were like walking into two very stiff "jabs" thrown by a heavyweight boxer. They hurt like shit but at least I had learnt the range of his reach and avoided being knocked out. Dr Chocolate-Love was right with the recovery speed of the operations. Each time I was out of hospital within two to three days. The pain was significant as the lung that had just been hacked into was still being used and moving while it was recovering. This meant that I felt each breath, cough or sneeze. In total I had lost around 30 percent of my lungs and unlike the liver, lungs do not grow back. They can, however, be trained to become more efficient.

By the looks of things this war was just about over. I had commanded my forces of medical strike teams, family, friends and support units across NSW and the Northern Territory. Battles had been fought throughout my body and there were definitely scars to remind me of what had occurred, what had once been reality and not just a bad dream. I had a month's rest before the final operation and I was anxious and impatient. I felt like I had run a marathon and now the final kilometres were all downhill. The final doctor to be recruited was to be a man whose personal battle would begin after we had met. The late Dr O'Brien will not be given a code name out of respect for him and what he did for so many cancer patients. Our paths met only briefly, but he left a lasting impression and I could only watch from the sidelines as his battle with cancer raged and eventually ended. I would not say, however, that he lost his battle, as from what I saw, he died a winner.

The lump that had been cut out of my neck back in Darwin had grown back over the last few months. In the process of removing the original tumour, a small (most probably microscopic) amount had been missed and had continued to increase. Doc Rabbit had explained to me some months earlier that this could occur and did not necessarily mean that malignant cancer had returned. I was informed that benign teratomas, consisting of live tissue and cells, could and usually did continue to grow, especially in my condition where the testicular cancer had been so aggressive. So we had to go back in and clear out this resurgent enemy a second and hopefully final time. Dr O'Brien was the best man for the job, as was explained to me by my numerous medical specialists. After meeting him for the pre-op consultation I was confident that this was going to be a relatively simple manoeuvre considering all that I had been through already. I do use the term simple very loosely. As a matter of fact, there did exist a fair degree of threat in this operation. The surgeon was going to cut into an area that had been operated on previously (always a tricky feat in the medical world), and the neck area consists of main arteries, veins and nerves that can be accidentally cut during the procedure, causing all kinds of problems. The ability of this enemy to reappear in territory where it had already been systematically defeated and removed was difficult for me to accept; another reminder that this enemy did not follow the conventional rules of conflict.

For what I hoped to be the final time I advanced into the hospital and underwent all the usual pre-op battle preparations. My support network and I were all confident and relaxed about this decisive hit. Mum and Dad didn't even come down as I assured them I would be out of hospital in record time. At the eleventh hour, however, as the tablet induced relaxant started to kick-in, I had a fearful moment that maybe I was being too confident, that maybe we had been complacent in the lead-up to this operation and that while my defences were down, the cancer would hit me with an unexpected counter-attack. I hadn't written a will this time or sufficiently said good-bye, no "just-in-cases". The Angel-Whisperer calmed me down and then, as if on cue, the nurses and ward attendant arrived to wheel my bed into battle.

The operation was successful with no unexpected complications. This was now my sixth operation within 14 months, all of them having some degree of complexity and seriousness. However, by either luck or good fortitude, I had never developed any complication, infection or fever, as if by act of will alone. My old adage "Doc, you do your job and let me worry about the rest," had held steady. This operation was performed at Strathfield Private and I was fortunate enough to have my own room. I woke up the following morning as the registrars did their rounds and I was astonished to hear that my stats were good and I would be able to go home the same day. I had enough time to have a shower and get dressed before the Angel-Whisperer would arrive. As yet she only thought she would be visiting, not taking me home. I shuffled into the bathroom, stripped off and had a shower.

I remember this moment clearly as if it were yesterday. I looked over and met myself in the mirror. The guy I saw was gaunt and tired-looking with a water-proof bandage strip covering the newest scar at the bottom of his neck. Without over-dramatising the moment, I leant back against the wall, covered my face with my hands and absolutely lost it. The tears that fell were 14 months worth of conflict, anguish and stress. I sobbed more at that moment than I had at any other time that I can recall and there was no way of stopping these tears until all the torment and realisation of what I had been through was out. This was the moment I had never actually prepared myself for during the whole ordeal. It was over, I was cured of this massive and debilitating disease.

Dealing with cancer for me had become somewhat easy. I had a defined illness/enemy with explainable signs and symptoms. This meant that I could steel myself with the determination to fight the illness during the hard time and resolve to get better. But now this moment had come, I was at a loss. An analogy of this feeling could be someone who had spent their life dedicated to fighting a vendetta only to find that the target of their energy and anger was now gone. What does one do with their life after they have fought so hard to keep it? I had no more doctors arranging the next surgery, no more rounds of chemo. In a second of realisation I had moved from cancer patient to cancer survivor. In an ironic twist that I think all cancer survivors experience, I found that after fighting so hard to be rid of this disease, I had now defined myself as a person with cancer. Who was I now that I no longer had cancer? Yes, having cancer was the easy part; it was surviving afterwards that was going to be a bitch.

# CHINA

*"Fame or integrity: which is more important?*
*Money or happiness: which is more valuable?*
*Success or failure: which is more destructive?*

*If you look to others for fulfillment,*
*You will never truly be fulfilled.*
*If your happiness depends on money,*
*You will never be happy with yourself.*

*Be content with what you have;*
*Rejoice in the way things are.*
*When you realise nothing is lacking,*
*The whole world belongs to you."*

LAO-TZU

The next 12 months passed with a lot less drama, except now each day for me seemed much more significant. I found myself running around trying to fit as much into life as I possibly could. Hector and I started each day with a walk through the bush tracks of Riverview that lined Sydney's Harbour Foreshore, and from there my days were spent doing various activities. I was determined to return to the exact same physical state as I was before the illness. I realised pretty quickly that this was going to take a long time as I was unable to do one push-up and going to the public indoor pool at Lane Cove saw me struggling to complete one lap of the pool without being completely breathless.

I found myself going back to Zhao and getting seriously into Qigong as a means of strengthening my inner energy. I signed up for one of his courses called the 12-cycles. This is a three-month course that comprises twelve exercises and daily meditation. It also requires you to abstain from coffee, alcohol and sex for three months. Considering that we were not in ancient China, Zhao allowed his students a little leniency with these rules, lucky as I was a soldier, not a monk!

The 12-cycle course is designed to strengthen inner energy and is suitable for people of any age and fitness level. Upon completion your results are manifested by the ability to perform feats that you would not think possible. These include chopping blocks of granite with the palm of your hand or on your forehead, breaking plastic chopsticks on the soft part of your throat (in the nook under your Adam's apple), and having stone pavers on your head or belly broken with a sledge hammer! This may all sound hard-core but it really is amazing to watch 60-plus-year-old women perform some of these and the surprise on their face afterwards. If you don't believe in the whole concept of energy forces within the body, these feats can be just as easily explained by accessing the power of the mind. Whichever way you explain it, I found this course did wonders for me physically as well as boosting my confidence. By the end of the 12 cycles I was jogging with Hector along our paths and was back to 30-40 push-ups. I still had a long way to go but this was a great start in my eyes.

I was still struggling to come to terms with what I had been through. At that time, as now, I had no idea what the cause of my cancer was. It could have been genetic or possibly as a result of Dad's exposure to Agent Orange during the Vietnam War. It may have been my exposure to high radio frequency emissions while in the Army. It may also have been simply from taking a hit to my nuts while playing rugby … did it really matter? I was confused and became paranoid about having a relapse. To an extent I became obsessed with all the things that we are told may cause cancer. I started eating organic food, stopped using a microwave and went to energetic healers so they could repair my "spiritual blueprint". The more I got into this lifestyle, the harder it became. If you start looking at our lifestyle, culture and diet, everything seems to be carcinogenic! Even the treatment of cancer causes cancer as the chemo they pump into you is poisonous. The peak of this paranoia came when I read a conspiracy theory that found medicine was second only to arms dealing as the largest global "business". It seems there will never be a cure for cancer as this would create a global economic collapse. Just think of all the businesses that rely on cancer research, technical development and treatment. Look at all the charities and fundraisers that are held every year across the world. I wondered why, after all the money raised and effort invested, the incidence of cancer diagnosis was still on the increase. It seemed to make very good sense to me reading all of this that we were all pawns in a global money-making conspiracy, and I became a believer.

My role as a soldier began to falter. I began walking an alternate path that although I didn't understand, it still made more sense than the military ethos I had adopted earlier. I started to look for a new career option. But what does a reformed war-fighter, ex-cancer patient *hippie* do for a living? At that time I hadn't discovered surfing.

In November 2003 I was right to go back to work. Although I had been unable to answer the questions above, and I was not really sure if I was still suited to the Army, I was eager to get working and return some normality to my life. Being able to go to work meant that I was no longer sick and it was a big landmark for me. I must have looked out of place on the bus heading into the city on that first day as the excitement and energy in my eyes surely could not have been associated with a skinny, gaunt bloke heading back to work in the military.

Going back to work had its problems as well as advantages. My paranoia subsided somewhat due to the distraction of everyday living. I was also able to exercise daily at the gym and this, combined with my walks and Qigong, began doing a good job of building my body back into a battle-ready state. Pride also played a big part in this. In my new job I had a Regimental Sergeant-Major who was nearing retirement age. Despite his years, this weathered soldier still completed the Army's annual fitness test, which included a 2.4 kilometre run to a time limit dependant on age. Being a 27-year-old captain trying to keep up with a 60-year-old warrant officer, and have him encourage me to continue, was ego shattering ... but motivating all the same.

One of the bigger problems I began to face was meeting up with old friends and associates and dealing with their reaction to what I had become.

"Wow Matt, you're a shadow of your former self!" Haven't you lost weight? You used to be massive," were common themes which again assisted in my feelings of displacement. Luckily I was to meet another senior soldier but still considerably younger than the one I introduced you to earlier, who had the patience and personality to "retrain" me into a soldier and Officer. Sully is one of those unique personalities who even in the military is hard to forget. He can sell ice to Eskimos, yell the spots off a leopard and at the same time give you the shirt off his own back. The job we were in was very much an office job and far removed from a typical Army regiment. It used to be classed as a respite posting, given to members at the end of their military career or in need of rest or medical recuperation. The problem with these postings is that it is easy to lose motivation. Sully and I leaned on each other to build and maintain a distinctive Army attitude, and I will always be grateful to this posting for introducing me to someone who has become such a good friend.

Despite the fact that my military career, health, fitness and life in general were all returning to an acceptable level, I was still feeling very lost and unsettled. My Qigong practice helped to an extent, but did not seem to be enough. I continued to search through the multitude of alternate therapies, treatments, tonics and latest fads. I was by now a vegetarian, almost a vegan. I ate only organic foods, no meat, dairy or sugar and drank no alcohol. I only allowed myself eggs as a form of maintaining decent protein levels for my weight training. I whole-heartedly attempted every version of cancer-fighting alternative treatment, but they had no effect. On my first check up scan, about eight months after I experienced that monumental emotional release in the shower, Dr Rather-be-Fishing had to tell me that the tumours had returned.

"Well they haven't really returned – they were always there, but they have grown from being very small and unnoticeable to ... bigger."

Shock, disbelief, fear and numbness all seemed to hit me at the same time. Doesn't quite sound possible does it? How could you be numb and still know in the background that all these emotions are jumping around not only your head, but your whole body, your whole being?

The blood results proved normal, which indicated that the malignant cancer had not returned. But the tumours had continued to grow under their own steam. Just like the tumor in my neck, some particles of the old disease had remained, hidden, and were gradually regaining strength. My war with cancer had moved from a conventional fight against an identifiable force into an insurgency. Insurgencies have occurred throughout history when one force destroys and occupies the territory of another force relatively quickly. The most recent, obvious and relevant cases of insurgencies are the conflicts in Iraq and Afghanistan.

"Where?" – Abdomen, chest and lungs. Everywhere we had already been ... shit. I had to give it to this disease, it was as stubborn as me.

With some pride I can say that I got over this shock relatively quickly and resolved to take positive action. My soldier's optimism told me the good news was that the cancer had not returned. I also had plenty of time as these masses were quite small and not posing any immediate threat. There was even a chance that they may not grow any further (a chance also that they would continue to grow and possibly turn cancerous again). I decided that I would apply all my newly acquired arsenal and knowledge in alternative treatment to fight these tumours. They would shrink and disappear via natural treatment, tumeric tablets, almond kernels (the latest things I was into at that time) and a good swig of my own piss each morning as advised by an alternative medicine scientist I had recently been to.

A further six months passed before I had another scan. I was definitely feeling and looking healthy, and I was confident that all this positive energy would have an effect on these little outposts of disease. In a scene that continually reminds me of the movie Groundhog Day, I went to the imaging centre got some CT scans and returned the following day for an appointment with Dr Rather-be-Fishing for a review of the results. This is always an emotional time. All the fear and doubt I had been able to suppress in the previous months return and I find myself anxious about what is happening inside me. Why do I need to get these doctors to run tests and tell me what is wrong with my own body? It doesn't seem right.

The second scan told a similar story to the first. The tumours were still there (no miraculous disappearing act here), but they showed little evidence of growth or activity.

"What do we do, Doc?" – I was at a loss myself. I really believed that all the alternate treatment, and money spent, would have affected these tumours. At the very least I had hoped for a slight reduction in size. Dr Rather-be-Fishing shared my indecisiveness. We could go back in and operate again (his slightly preferred option), or, we could do nothing and continue to wait (surprisingly my preferred option). I say surprisingly because it reflected a significant shift in my mentality and attitude. My younger self would have waded in for another fight without hesitation. The last two years, however, had taken their toll on me and I was buggered. I needed to rest and avoid another serious confrontation. I was opting for a typical military manoeuvre known as a "delaying action". I wanted to do what I could to stop or slow any progress of the enemy whilst avoiding a big fight until I was ready. Now this action is not a bad option, and is actually quite smart if you are weaker than the enemy or not on the ground of your choosing for battle, but it is defensive and I had always been an offensive type of guy …

Dr Rather-be-Fishing and I finally agreed that we would continue to wait, and watch. The abdominal operation had been massive. Going into the same area a second time posed some serious threats to my health and recovery. Due to its complexity, the next operation would be even bigger than before. Leaving the tumours could kill me, so could the operation to remove them – just my average Wednesday afternoon doctor's appointment. This reminded me how lucky I was to have a specialist like him on my side. Our discussions were always frank and honest and developing alongside our professional medical relationship was a genuine friendship and respect. With scans and blood tests every six months, any advance made by the tumours would be detected, and could be acted upon if required, without posing any further threat than they already did.

I write this all matter-of-factly, and as is my nature, this is how I deal with serious and emotional issues. But underneath this soldier's simplicity was turmoil. Partly because I was not good at waiting (the patience I have mentioned earlier is an ongoing development), but mostly because I was still struggling with identifying who I was now. I didn't technically have cancer, but neither was I healthy and carefree. With all I had tried that didn't work what now could I do to be proactive? Waiting shouldn't mean do nothing.

I decided it was time to go international. I would go to China, and train in Martial arts with the monks – this war was just about to go esoteric.

My reasoning to go to China was multi-layered, but it seemed to happen very naturally. First, my affinity with Qigong and Martial Arts painted China as a mystical and adventurous place where I could gain further insight into myself and this whole "energetic" phenomenon. Secondly, If I was going to feel lost and out of place when I was surrounded by friends, family and all that was familiar, then maybe I would be able to find myself in a place that was strange and unfamiliar where I actually was out of place. Thirdly, the Angel-Whisperer and I needed a break.

It seemed that as I recovered from the initial fight with cancer and my life returned to some normality, our relationship deteriorated. We didn't fight and argue, but we were definitely going in two different directions. I was going to China to get away from everything and everyone, and I think both of us knew that our time together was drawing to an end.

I did some research on the internet and found a Kung Fu school located in the North Eastern Corner of China (just above the North Korean Border). Naturally, going to such a location, while having a military background and particular security clearances, presented some problems, so I was required to get clearance and special briefings from Defence before making any bookings. Once it is was clear that I was not going to play James Bond, I was given the green light. My intent was to go to a Shaolin training academy for three months. I had no real intention to travel around as I believed there would be enough of that going on inside my head. Also, three months under the one instructor, although not so long in the Martial arts world, would be better than shorter periods under multiple instructors. I had no real idea what to expect. I had not met anyone who had done a similar thing so I felt like I was in an old Kung Fu movie with me seeking out an ancient Chinese Master (long whispy grey chin beard and all). Once found, he would have me doing all kinds of ridiculous exercises with meanings I only grasp overtime and awakened wisdom. I decided I would write a journal, making entries each day to record this journey. I had never been into keeping diaries in the past and so this was going to be all about me doing new things. Mum bought me a journal as a farewell gift and I arranged to have a bit of a party before I left, this really gave the trip an air of adventure and excitement.

So it was on a cool day at the beginning of July that I farewelled the Angel-Whisperer at Sydney International airport and walked through the customs gates. This had also been the first time in over three years that I was going somewhere "alone" – no relatives or friends or medical support. The best way to describe how I was feeling at the time is to relay the first entry of my journal;

DAY 1 - 02 Jul 04

*Sitting on the plane. I have just said goodbye to all that I love and I am now waiting for the plane to take off, land, and catch up* with my soul.

I currently feel really excited and restless. I was sad to say good-bye to (Angel-Whisperer), she felt really small and fragile in my arms. I guess that is part of the reason why it is good that I am going. I have already decided that I will get either a pencil or finer pen for this log. My hand writing is bad enough.

Wheels are moving! The hostesses are spieling off instructions in Japanese (I flew JAL for that trip). I remember the words but not the meaning. Old memories of my trip to Japan are filling me now. On that journey I developed so, and now I am off again to rebuild and find what died and what was reborn during my illness with cancer.

Already the words are starting to literally fall out of my head. Annie (An awesome lady who was treating me with Bowan Therapy), was right "don't take books!" she had said – "write. For god's sake write". She had continued to say that books would only distract me where as writing this journal would encourage me to go within - funny how close "journal" is to "journey"...

The plane is empty, I am sitting alone, rather symbolic. I think this may be the start of a book – "The Kung Fu of Cancer!"…. Shit I can't stop writing/thinking. The Angel-Whisperer wanted to buy me a journal but I said no because Mum and Annie had already bought me one each. Now I'm thinking that I could have easily used three. We are still on the runway and everything I see is symbolic or relevant to this journey. The world is suddenly communicating my thoughts in a coherent way. I'll give a great example – I had just put the book down to relax my hand, and thoughts. As mentioned, both are moving faster than this jet could *ever wish to move, and my eyes fall onto the monitor above the aisle. It is showing a camera view just below the nose of the plane. The picture is live footage of the runway and I, along with anyone else who has ever flown, have seen this before. But I never really saw the point of it. You can't see anything except the runway directly ahead, and a flirting horizon. But isn't that all I see in life? I know my destination (or think I do... ) – Japan, China, old age! And I know where I boarded from. I feel this plane's flight with all its bumps and rattles and the drone of air-con. I can even see the airspeed and progress on the screen. But I don't really have control over this journey. All I can do is enjoy the ride and some of the in-flight beverages.*

*Acceleration, a surge in g-force, a surge in the belly and then we are airborne. The camera is still on and relays a picture of us flying/ floating over Sydney, similar to a movie scene when the camera does a first-person shot during the death of a character – floating away from the world. I never thought of flying in this way before and now that I am in the clouds I will sit and wait, scratch and fidget, watch a movie or 5 and play Tetris, while this journey/plane/next three months continues along its path. I'll wait for that next violent re-connection with the earth...*

I was picked up from the airport by a friend of Zhao and shown around Beijing for the day. My train for the North, to a city named Siping, Hubei province, did not depart until that evening so we had the day to travel around the smoggy capital exploring some markets and Tiananmen Square. Everything in China was new and amazing to me. It is an incredibly busy and industrialised place, yet at the same time, there are groups of citizens practising Tai Chi with swords on every available piece of grass. China seems to be a societal impact zone in the clash between technology and antiquity. Brand new Lexus cars will overtake donkey-drawn carts along roads that change between bitumen, dirt and tiles. It is also immensely large. The train ride was about nine hours long, a relatively short trip for China. I arrived in the early morning to be met at the station by representatives of the Siping Shaolin Kung Fu Academy.

The school is about 30 minutes' drive out of Siping City, set amongst some tiny rural villages that are surrounded by fields of corn, the main crop in this fairly poor region. Siping City itself is a very small city with about 5 million people. The school is upon a hill overlooking a valley and lake and is very picturesque, although I found out quickly that it was built with the intention of catering for foreigners. This essentially meant that it was very commercial and profit-orientated, a detail that was disappointing to me as I had hoped for oriental insight and seclusion. This also meant that most students were foreigners (mainly from Australia, America and Europe), the recreation room had couches and a TV/DVD player with constant showings of pirated, new release movies bought from the local markets and a small restaurant/bar just at the gates that served chips and burgers along with the local cuisine, and held a large stock of beer and spirits, all at only slightly inflated prices (a long-neck beer would set you back around $1 AUD).

The training routine consisted of a six-day training week, with Sunday off. Needless to say the aforementioned restaurant got a hammering on Saturday nights by the foreigners. A normal training day would look something like this;

*MON-SAT*
*0600 - A run down to the main road and then back up the hill*
*(approx 3 kilometres)*
*0700 - Morning QI Gong*
*0800 – Breakfast*
*0900 to 1130 - Martial arts training (either Shaolin Kung Fu or*
*    "Taji/Tai Chi")*
*1200 to 1500 – Lunch and afternoon rest*
*1500 to 1730 – Martial arts training (except Saturdays where*
*    the day finishes at lunch)*
*1800 – Dinner.*

It was a pretty intense day of training especially if you were participating in the Shaolin Classes, considered a "hard" martial art in the sense that it focuses more on physical strength and fitness and is very much a younger person's art. The Taji/Tai Chi classes are "soft" and require much more development of inner energy and relaxation in order to become skilful. Your average Chinese Martial Artist will start studying at one of these schools at 5-6 years of age old and will have academic lessons mixed into the daily program. They will study at one of these schools until they are 18-20 years' old and mainly focus on a "hard" system of martial art. Upon graduation they go out into the workforce, or join the military, or are chosen as an instructor and continue training. It is not until the age of 30-plus that they begin to study a "softer" system.

I originally intended to take the Shaolin classes for the duration of my stay, partly because I had done so in the past, partly because my ego believed I should be training in a "hard" system and partly because I was obsessed with becoming as fit and robust as I was before my disease.

Time is a funny thing, when you are happy and well – it passes very quickly. When you are sad and in pain – it passes very, very slowly. The first week of my training took a very long time to finish, and I was having an extremely hard time walking by the end of it. Being an Australian soldier I felt I had to do everything at a harder and more intense level than any of the other students, regardless of their age, fitness or skill level. This training, however, was very specific and not like anything I had done before. Those little Chinese instructors broke the shit out of me that week as if I was the youngest and greenest recruit. Luckily the pain I was going through was not uncommon to the other foreign students and on the Saturday afternoon I was bundled into a small taxi with three wheels and taken into Siping City, and the Pink Palace.

The Pink Palace is aptly named because the building is painted bright pink and stands out distinctly among the grey industrial buildings of Communist China. I don't know the proper way to describe this establishment but perhaps it can be best placed as an adult recreational and leisure facility. It is part motel, part day spa and part massage parlour (in both the legitimate and shady term). The Pink Palace was particularly popular amongst the foreign students training at the academy as it had a very large and extensive hot bath section. There were pools of different temperature ranging from 12 degrees through to 40. We would alternate between each of them sending our muscles through the complete range of extremes. There were also sauna and steam rooms and salt massages. After an hour of this luxurious punishment, we would head upstairs to a common motel room where we would order room service and watch satellite TV. This was not what I had expected when coming to China for a monk-like existence and spartan solitude. But fuck it felt good.

After the initial shock of the training schedule, my body adjusted and my fitness improved. I was enjoying myself and the company of the other students (from all walks of life, age and motivation), but I knew that I was not getting what I needed from this journey. Although the physical side of training was good, I was not going "inside" as I had hoped. I decided to change over to the Taji/Tai Chi classes and shift focus. For one thing the instructor of this class was somewhat of the real deal. God only knows how old he was (80-plus years), but his distinguishing achievement was as a personal bodyguard to Chairman Mao Zedong! He didn't speak too much, and what he did say was conveyed through a translator, but his skills and ability could be easily understood as could his strength when giving a demonstration. One of the other students claimed to have seen him hurl a handful of nails at a plank of wood and have all of them drive in point-first. I'm sure Mao's bodyguards would have been armed with hardware more substantial than nails, but this was still a very impressive feat.

The training in the "softer" system began to have the desired effect. That, along with my daily Qigong exercises allowed my mind to start slowing down and relax. This was significant as I had not realised how anxious I had become from fighting cancer. I realised that ever since the last round of operations I had been in a race to reclaim lost time and youth. I started to realise that I was never going to be exactly like I was before I was diagnosed, but that this was not necessarily a bad thing. It just was.

I was enjoying this simple existence of training, resting,

eating (and the occasional drinking), and had met some good friends. I had all but temporarily forgotten who I was back in Australia when the academy had some surprise visitors. We had just started our morning class when an Army jeep drove up the hill with four green-clad occupants. My senses were awakened instantly as I knew there could not be too many reasons why these men would be here. After initially calling into the administration office, all four drove around to the training courtyard in which I was practicing and parked the jeep. My inner-calm was dislodged somewhat as I attempted to continue my slow meditative movements, all the while, being under the not-so-discrete glare of these soldiers. When I was being briefed by the Army prior to departing, I was warned that I may be supervised or investigated while in China. I was also told that I should not attempt to do anything but allow this to occur and be compliant with anything that was asked of me.

Lunch time came and I scurried off to the food hall and made idle conversation with my friends. These soldiers were the talk of the day as no-one had ever seen this before, and the question of why they were here was bantered around. Unfortunately when I returned to the courtyard for the afternoon session, they were still there. I remember wondering if I should ask these gents how they could be so bored that they had nothing better to do than watch some hairy westerner attempt to do Tai Chi and obviously disrupt my serenity, but thought better of it. They drove off around 1700 that day without having ever spoken a word to me, just letting me know they were there I guess.

My training continued and I could definitely notice improvements, especially in my flexibility and power, although

I was enjoying myself, I was still restless inside with the feeling that I was not in the right place. Two more events occurred in this same week which had a significant impact on my journey.

I had been in contact with everyone back home via email and the occasional telephone call. After a phone conversation one day with the Angel-Whisperer, it was officially decided that it was time to break up. I think we were both expecting it but were delaying the event until after I had left. We agreed that she would stay in our rented house (we had moved from Riverview to Lindfield just prior to my departure), and would look after Hector until I got back. I had now effectively shed that emotional attachment and was able to totally focus on me and this sojourn. This may sound callous but I am a firm believer that someone cannot truly be happy or in-love with another person unless they are happy or in-love with themselves first. Otherwise you are just using the other person to fill a void. I was still trying to work out who I had now become and to do this I needed to be alone, without the emotional support or presence of anyone else. I emailed my family and close friends to let them know what was happening, strangely enough there were not too many of them who showed surprise.

The second event was the return of some students who had taken a month off training to travel the country. They had some awesome tales to tell and mentioned a school they had visited on Wudang Mountain in the province of Hubei. Wudang is believed by many to be the birth-place of Tai Chi and is one of the sacred epicenters of Tao-ism. Anyone who has seen the movie *Crouching Tiger Hidden Dragon*, will remember it well (although an interesting note is that the location in the movie is very different to the actual mountain). This struck a chord in me for some reason and I decided instantly that it was time for me to go and seek out this mountain. I had not intended to travel on this trip, nor had I intended to be watching reruns of *Friends* each night with German backpackers. But I had never intended to get cancer, either.

The lesson here was that things never seem to turn out how we expect them to and that sometimes you've just to roll with things. There were a few other students who mentioned their desire to travel, but were not keen on doing it alone (especially a Swedish girl named Eva traveling for the first time out of Europe on her own and feeling a little out of her depth, and who ended up adopting me as her big hairy brother). We needed to wait a week or two for the school to arrange a refund of our advance payment (we were actually lucky to get any money back from them at all), and this gave us time to make some plans for the trip. So after spending roughly a month in the Academy in Northern China I set off again south to Beijing, after one last stop at the Pink Palace for our last taste of luxury.

We had arranged to stay at the Workers Stadium, which was a major football/sports stadium with a backpackers lodge located inside. There were four of us that had left the academy and we spent a week in Beijing before heading south-west into the centre of China. I was still determined to continue my practice so I got up each morning and trained in the park with millions of others across the country and even found the odd tree to hit as a part of conditioning training. I was still meditating each day but this was a lot harder in the city with so many distractions. Through the day we checked out various tourist attractions including the Great Wall, the Emperor's Summer Palace and the Forbidden City. The little part of Beijing that could be classed as the "night-life" region was also frequented and I'll admit that I also found that I was enjoying being single again.

Soon enough though my feet were getting itchy and I made plans to head to the Wudang Mountain range. Eva wanted to come along and so did a Canadian guy who was courting her at the time. We bought three tickets and begun preparations.

The train ride to Wudang was about 15 hours, which went surprisingly well as we boarded with hangovers and were able to sleep the majority of the way. A good tip for travelers though; as in other Asian countries many of the trains in China have toilets that "flush" straight onto the track. So make sure you hang on to anything you want to keep when relieving yourself. It is easy to lose the odd pair of sunglasses or loose pocket change. For me it was the sunglasses. We decided to break up the trip by visiting the city of Shaolin. This is where the original Shaolin Buddhist Temple was located. Although there is a temple there now for tourists to visit, and to be fair, with monks still practising religion and their Kung Fu, the original temple had been burned down and rebuilt a number of times over the centuries by nervous emperors and invading armies. The town is home to scores of Martial arts schools all offering the teachings of authentic Shaolin Kung Fu and there are literally thousands of students, Chinese and foreign, out in the training squares going through their exercises throughout the day. I realised that the "spiritual" escape I had been searching for may be more elusive than I first anticipated. Shaolin was famous worldwide, as was Wudang. Perhaps this would be what was awaiting me at my next destination – A Lego-city of toy soldiers all selling an authentic art that isn't really authentic. The following day we boarded another train and headed for Hubei province.

The Wudang Mountain Range is quite large, about 400 square kilometres. Again, this area of China is poor and the village at the foot of the mountains was nothing like that of Shaolin, thankfully. We had no idea where to go, who to ask, or what we were really looking for so we hired a room in a hotel near the train station and set out to look for someone who spoke a little English. As strange as it sounds, I was relieved to find it difficult to find anyone who spoke English. This meant that there would not be too many commercial martial art schools in the area. We had a little translator pocket-book and this was sufficient to order us food and ask about training schools. The few we found in town were similar to the one we had just left except there were no foreigners training here, although the administrators were excited at the prospect of training us. We could see their eyes counting the US dollars we would be paying. We delayed making a decision for a day or so and decided to travel up to the sacred mountain first.

As yet we had not seen the actual Wudang Mountain as it had been extremely foggy. We hired a taxi and headed out of town, through a parkland's control gate and then started a steep ascent. I remember being surprised at how steep the road was and how lush the mountainous forest was. Until now, I had seen little actual Chinese bushland as all the areas I had traveled through were cultivated. This, however, started to look like the China I had imagined. We continued to drive higher and it was impossible to see beyond the next bend in the road let alone the summit. I began to realise the fog we were going in and out of was actually cloud. The taxi driver knew we were on the lookout for a Kung Fu school and when we were close to the top of the ranges, we pulled off the road and into what appeared to be an old motel, with a faded sign above the entrance the Wudang Wu-shu Academy. This definitely was not dolled up for the foreign dollar and it was so enshrouded by clouds it was hard to tell if it was actually inhabited. We were welcomed in by the administrators and seated in a foyer. There were a few foreigners training here and they came in to meet us and check us out. This place had a peculiar feel and actually felt like we were being interviewed by these students. After some general conversation they seemed to warm to us and explained how the school worked and what price we should pay when negotiations began with the monks.

"Monks?" I asked sceptically. Until now I had only met Chinese martial arts instructors who claimed to be monks, or to have visited a Buddhist monastery some time in their childhood.

"Yes. The instructors here are all Tao-ist monks from the mountain monastery up the road. They each have at least 20 years of Tao-ist instruction," replied Wes, a charismatic young American who had now been here for almost 12 months. This was sounding promising.

Our first impressions were good so after negotiating a price for training with the monks, we headed back down to the village to collect our bags from the motel.

The teachings of Tao are very different from those of Buddhism. Whereas Buddhists follow scriptures and strict regimes in their search for enlightenment, Taoists are more relaxed, believing that each person must find and follow their own path to enlightenment. Therefore various Taoists have taken some very different paths, including alcohol, sex and seclusion as their particular direction. Therefore the training at this academy was different to that of the Shaolin academies around China. Instead of being told the forms/style I was to be taught, I chose them myself. I decided upon a little known system, spelled by some *Hsing-Yi*. This was a very simple system designed by a Chinese General a few hundred years ago and centred on five specific strikes, each one a counter strike to the one before. I also chose to be taught Qigong by these monks and in particular a technique called Iron Shirt. This involved various breathing and physical exercises which allowed you to centre your energy and focus on parts of your body and stop it from being hurt when struck. The training was also less intense with the students setting their own pace and the monks watching on and instructing when required. Down time was spent meditating and walking along the various mountain tracks.

The accommodation was also very "interesting". This academy was located in an old hotel and so the rooms were hotel rooms with en-suites. However, there was no running water in the bathrooms except for the toilet which occasionally flushed. Therefore we were required to carry water in buckets, collected from the taps on the first floor, up to our 4th floor rooms. If the flushing was offline, we would pour a bucket of water into the bowl. Washing consisted of a "bird-bath" in the tub or shower recess. Hot water boiled from the jug was optional. The accommodation was very basic and brilliant. This was just what I had been looking for. The food, unlike the accommodation, was excellent. Meals were included in the training package and for 90 percent of my time in China I had no idea what I was eating. The cooks at this school took a lot of pride in what they created. Whatever it was, it tasted great.

All the foreign students (roughly nine), had chosen

different things to learn and we all trained in the same area at around the same time. This was mainly because the translator would be around to tell us what the monks were saying. We created a very tight little community and often went on bush walks or traveled into the village to check emails or buy supplies. Our rest days were Thursdays and this meant that we had to be on our guard Wednesday nights. The monks were prone to getting drunk on this night and would proceed to "test" our skills once they had a skinfull. These guys were all quite small and usually weighed about 65 kilograms, but when they hit you, it was like being slammed by an angry elephant.

About three weeks into our stay we were taken on a bushwalk by two of the monks. We needed to take packs with overnight supplies as we would not be returning until the end of the following day. We headed off into the mountains following a small dirt track, which was often hard to discern amongst the foliage. Our destination was the Temple of Five Dragons, a very old and sacred temple that had been visited by emperors over the last couple of thousand years to pray and meditate. We had not timed our walk very well as we were still trekking as the sun dropped below the mountains and visibility started to get really bad. We were often walking along the top of cliffs and the thought of one of us going over the edge, out here in the middle of the wilderness was not enticing.

The temple had been in ruins for some time now and there was no road directly to it. We arrived on the outskirts just as the last hint of daylight was lost behind ominous peaks. Despite being in ruins, and having no service road attached to the temple (the nearest village with a road was 30 minutes walk), a small group of Taoist Monks lived here and tended to the temple. Upon arrival, we were required to meditate/ pray in the temple with the monks and then were invited to dine with them. These practising monks were vegetarian and grew their own vegetables along the old terraces of the temple ruins. The whole place resembled something out of a Lara Croft Tomb Raider movie. The food they cooked for us was astonishingly good and mainly consisted of eggplant, noodles and cucumbers. We slept in bunks that night and we all commented on how peaceful our night's sleep had been. I found out the next morning that our room had been the Emperor's concubine quarters. We got up early to practise our exercises in the temple grounds, before giving a donation and thanks to the monks and heading off. I was musing on how serene and timeless this old temple was and how secluded from the world these monks were as we walked past their residence and noticed on the shackled roof a satellite TV dish! Such are the luxuries of the modern day I guess – even for monks.

We returned to the academy via a different route, which took us the rest of the day to travel, visiting small, forgotten shrines along the way. I was exhausted by the time I got back but felt exhilarated at the same time. This was the China I had come to visit and these were the experiences that were helping me rediscover myself.

At home in Australia, I had an event in Darwin I was planning to attend after my trip. By now Mum was heavily involved in the Cancer Council for the Northern Territory and they were holding a fundraising charity night with a world famous pianist performing. I had been asked to be MC and guest speaker for the night and was expected to have a speech prepared. Although I am not at all uncomfortable with public speaking, this would be my first time since my illness.

In addition, I would be required to speak directly about my illness. This was going to be an honour, but confronting. The question had been lingering in the back of my mind "What the fuck am I going to talk about?" but I had been unable to come to an answer. I was still writing regularly in my journal, and my time on Wudang had seen my thoughts becoming more philosophical. There was less questioning and confusion, and more acceptance and happiness. One day I started writing with no particular direction and after completing 2-3 pages, I realised that I had written my speech. It was more of a reflection than a speech, but it spoke of my thoughts on a life-threatening disease, and the life this disease had given me. I titled it *The Rose Bush* and then forgot about it until several months later when I was preparing for the night in Darwin.

I had spent almost four weeks on Wudang, but had not yet climbed to the summit, so a group of us arranged to go up the next Thursday. The summit of Wudang is a single peak that overlooks the entire mountain range. It also houses a complex of temples and residences built into the mountain side. Like so many tourist sites, there is the traditional way of getting to this attraction, which in this case consisted of roughly 10,000 steps (I can't confirm this as I lost count after about 43, but it definitely felt like 10,000), or there is the convenient way – a cable car. Being young, adventurous and with spiritual purpose, we set off up the stairs. It took us about three hours to reach the summit's temple complex. As we were climbing, one of the veteran students recounted an event 12 months prior when one of our teachers – Su-Sifu (Sifu being the Chinese word for father or teacher) was called up to the mountain temple by one of the older monks. He ran the stairs and arrived within the hour!

We rested at one of the restaurants and had some green tea and noodles and watched other people arrive either via the stairs like us, or energetically de-boarding the cable cars. I am not knocking Chinese engineering, but I was happy to have taken the long road up as opposed to sitting in one of those cars and being suspended hundreds of metres above a mountain range…

At the time I was twenty-eight. What amazed me most about the people on this mountain was not the monks, but the labourers who had the job of carrying bags of sand up the hill. There was work being done constantly on the up-keep of this tourist attraction and this work required mortar, cement and soil. For some reason the cable cars were not an option and the only other way up here was the stairs. So these gents, aged from 15-70, would spend their days walking up and down the mountain with sandbags suspended on a carry stick positioned across their shoulders with a nook in the middle for neck comfort. Their legs were like iron cables and they usually had a cigarette hanging out of their mouths. Their pay would only be the equivalent of a few dollars per trip.

After the rest we were ready for the final ascent. The temple complex was built similar to a fortress with walls surrounding the peak of the mountain and a main gate guarded by ticket collectors. We walked and climbed along spiral corridors and alleyways smiling at the local monks and checking out different artifacts until we reached the final stairway. My legs were burning by this stage and I wished that I had another lung, but this part of the climb was relatively short, and without warning I stumbled onto the top of the mountain. I didn't really know what to expect. I hadn't done a lot of mountain climbing or trekking before, but this view took what little breath I had away.

The absolute top of Wudang has been flattened and turned into an open air altar. It is around 20 metres x 20 metres and ringed by a small iron chain fence. The chain has thousands of padlocks attached to it by visitors who have made a wish and locked them in for eternity. The platform falls away dramatically from the fence down a hundred metres and is met by the roofs and cobble stoned pathways of the temple complex. For 360 degrees there is an uninterrupted view of this Chinese mountain range, green and misty. This was the culmination of my trip and just as in the shower, thousands of kilometres away, thousands of hours away, in Strathfield Private Hospital, I cried with relief that I had lived to be in this moment. Luckily, the only hot chick in the area was Eva and she was off the cards anyway so I didn't embarrass myself too much. Not that anyone would have been able to tell the difference between my tears and the streams of sweat falling from my forehead caused by the late summer heat and the exertion of the day's climb. I was just some tall, hairy, bearded Westerner dripping at the top of a mountain. The Chinese tourists and monks carried on without giving me any thought. I promised myself I would return here one day with my wife and family to show them a moment and place in time that had given me a spiritual centre. I actually had an idea who that wife may be. But, for now, it was time to start heading home.

The trip down was significantly quicker, although there was still a fair amount of strain on your legs descending 10,000 steps, especially when you are trying not to fall down the almost vertical decline. We made it back to the academy in time for dinner and we ate, and drank, to the day's achievements.

I had been in China for about three months and this

journey was drawing to an end. I didn't want to leave but knew I had to. I intended to go home and wrap up my life in Australia, get discharged from the Army and return to this place for a few more years of training. But that was in the future and I wasn't about to look too far into that window. Life had taught me that shit will happen to you without warning, and learning to adapt to things is a good quality to have. Accepting the present was much more enjoyable than worrying about the future or mourning the past. I had one more week of training, and was then heading to Beijing Airport. Eva was going to continue traveling with one of the guys into central China. I had become very good friends with a big tall black British guy named Oliver, whose trip to China was a 21st birthday present to himself. He was studying classical literature in London and needed to get back before next semester, so he and I were going to travel together back to Beijing. We made a pretty interesting pair walking around this country and often attracted extended stares from the locals.

I had also developed a good friendship, and respect for one of our teachers – Su-Sifu. He had taken an interest in my training and meditations and decided he should test my skills before I left. I had been training Iron Shirt, and as mentioned the monks had developed power in their punches that exceeded anything a heavyweight boxer could muster. He motioned to my abdomen and gave me time to concentrate my energy. This made me a little nervous as he was preparing to strike me just below the belly button and directly on the scar line where the surgery had been. His eyes though reassured me that I was ready for the test. He warmed up with a strike that would not bother too many people. The second thumped in significantly harder and had the force equivalent to that of a rugby front rower's shoulder coming in for a tackle. I felt no pain as his fist bounced off.

"Ready?" he asked with a thick accent.

I just nodded and focused as he had taught me.

The third punch landed with the force of a steam train. His body had whipped around so quickly that I didn't even see the strike launch. He pounded his fist into my flesh without mercy, but only penetrating a centimeter or two before bouncing back off, not harmlessly but also not harming. My body rocked back slightly under the force but I had repelled his strike and he looked at me with pride. The others applauded as they had all gathered around to watch. Wes later told me that he had diarrhea for a week after a similar test. I had learned a lot. Oliver and I hopped on the train the following day.

# DEE WHY

China had changed me physically as well as mentally. I had been there for three months during the Asian summer, and after training outdoors for six hours a day, I was brown, lean and bearded. Mentally, I was now at ease with who I was and what I had been through, and at the same time, the repetitive meditation and style of training had improved my focus and self-discipline. The biggest change in my perspective was that I felt like I was over the cancer, and that I could now move on with life and be free of this burdensome disease. I saw cancer as a wake-up call that I wasn't going to ignore, but I had a life that wasn't going to be wasted. As far as my place in the Army was concerned I realised that there was a hell-of-a-lot more in life outside the Army that I wanted to do. The Army had played a big part in creating who I was, but it is a very consuming vocation and it was time to be away from that environment, for a while at least. My plan was to return to Sydney, and the Army until the following year. I would save up some money and apply to take extended leave without pay and head back to Wudang the following Spring.

I arrived back in Sydney to a house that had been vacated by the Angel-Whisperer the previous day. Hector had been fed and was waiting out the back. This was an emotional reunion and I had a lot of calls to make and people to see, but that could all wait. Hector and I went for a walk.

Dad came down from Tweed Heads for a few days and we visited Manly beach to enjoy the sun and sand. I was renting a large three bedroom house in Lindfield, and the only reason left validating this location was the backyard for Hector. Dad suggested that it might be worth considering moving to a small apartment near the beach and where I could learn to enjoy Sydney. This was a great idea except for the fact that Hector now weighed about 75 kilograms and wouldn't do well in an apartment. I put this thought to the back of my mind to mull over for a while.

Now would be a good time to tell you about how my father's obsession with lawn bowls was born. Up until now Dad had not really been into a retirement sport. He played tennis once a week and had an active lifestyle up in Tweed Heads, but there was nothing to give his week routine. During his visit to Sydney, we decided to walk up to the West Lindfield

Bowling Club for a "social" roll-up. I have played the game maybe three times in my life so I had no pre-conceptions about my ability. Dad had not played too often himself, but what I had failed to realise in all these years was just how competitive my father is. As the game progressed, so did our focus. A competitive streak developed due to the tension of the game and the neck-to-neck score. It came down to the final roll and I finished up beating Dad by about two points. We laughed off the tension and went for a few beers. I had forgotten about the incident until I spoke to Dad a couple of weeks later. He had signed up with one of the major Tweed Heads bowling clubs and was getting some professional lessons. I guess there was no way he was going to let his young bull beat him in a game of bowls ever again. Dad now "rolls" three times a week and plays pennants. We've had a few games since in which he has gotten the better of me. But I am proud to say that it was the flogging he received at my hands that has driven him to be so good at his new hobby.

Soon after Dad's visit, I came up with a solution to my housing situation. If I was going to travel again, I would need to find an appropriate home for Hector. In my eyes there was only one place where I would be comfortable leaving him and it was practically a second home to him anyway. I rang up Mum and asked if Hector could move in with them in Darwin. There was no hesitation in her reply and we agreed that I could bring him up with me for the fundraising event in November. This gave me a workable timeframe to also find a new place. I started the search immediately and called in the assistance of a very good friend I had made through Qi gong – Lou. She knew the Northern Beaches area very well and had some experience in looking for real estate. We set up a date to check out available apartments along Manly beach.

The places available at the time were not good. I thought I had pretty simple requirements; close to the beach, easy to maintain, good access to the ferry. We were unable to find anything that felt right for me. Lou had mentioned Dee Why as an option and I had dismissed it due to the fact that it was too far away from the ferry. She can be tricky when she wants to be, and suggested we go there for lunch anyway – around the same time that there happened to be an open showing for a place she had seen advertised. I gave in and allowed myself to be led to this apartment located along the foreshore of Dee Why beach. It had an awesome balcony looking north up to Long Reef, and I fell in love with it straight away. I filled out the application on the spot and then allowed Lou to reel off the "I told you so" speech all the way back to Lindfield.

Everything seemed to be falling into place. I returned to work and started to pack up my things in Lindfield even before my application for Dee Why was approved. Hector and I flew up to Darwin for the Cancer Council fundraising evening and I realised that this was my first return to Darwin since I had left for Sydney and the operations. I had a feeling of closure and that my journey was now complete. I had not forgotten about the remaining tumours in my abdomen and chest and disappointingly, the scans I underwent post-China showed no reduction in their size. However, I could not ignore a sense of triumph. Surely I had seen the last of this disease? There is a general consensus, that if there is no relapse of cancer within five years of treatment, then there is a good likelihood that the disease has been successfully eliminated. It had been over two years since the last of the chemotherapy poison had conducted its clearing patrol through my veins, arteries and organs. There was no looking back for me now!

In Darwin, Gordon, some family friends, and I went fishing and mud crabbing. I visited some of my mates working at Robertson Barracks, went to the Saturday morning Parap markets for breakfast and generally soaked up the ambience of our northern-most city. I sat down to prepare my speech for the fundraising evening and for the first time since being in China, read over my journal entry in which I had written *The Rose Bush*. I tidied up the usual Matt Carr spelling mistakes and grammatical errors, but for the most part, the speech remained the same as it had been in Wudang.

The evening began and all was going well. I was enjoying myself as an MC of such an auspicious occasion. I ensured that I didn't drink too much as I needed my humour to stay on the right side of crass. Although I couldn't help making an obvious Freudian slip when I introduced the internationally acclaimed master "penis" (pianist), who had been flown in for the evening. The time came for me to give my speech. I gave the audience a quick up-date on who I was and what I had been through and then read out *The Rose Bush*. Up until then I felt that I had written something that was special to me. I had not rehearsed it and I had no idea if it was interesting or even made sense to anyone else. I completed the final sentence and looked up from my pages. I wasn't sure what I was expecting, but I hadn't counted on silence … I thought it best to let everyone know that this was the end of my speech. The quiet stand-off continued and I started to feel awkward. Some clapping did begin but then as I was able to focus on the crowd I realised with surprise that many people were crying! If it had been just the blokes crying I may have taken that as a sign that the speech had been as boring as crap, but it seemed like many people had something 'lodged in their eyes'. Eventually the clapping turned into applause and it dawned on me that I had been able to express my journey to an audience of people, the majority of whom I did not know, and a connection had been made. It seemed that what I had been through was somehow now validated. I sensed that the speech could perhaps help one or two of these audience members deal with a disease that would eventually affect all of them either directly or indirectly. This moment probably gave me the equivalent of $10,000 of therapy hours, and it felt good. There was nothing left of this night but for me to get drunk in Mitchell Street with my mate Morrie who was meeting up with me in about 30 minutes.

## The Rose Bush

*What If I hadn't survived? What of those people who don't wake up after that operation or are sent home with no more hope of treatment and cure? This is a point that we are all scared to discuss. Why? Death is just change, a very permanent change that we have absolutely no way of reversing or rectifying, but change just the same. How can I talk of accepting the change that death brings to someone who has experienced the debilitating grasp on life cancer secures as it grips onto a mother, father, partner or child?*

*I remember quite clearly the nights before those operations which have always marked the front-line of my battle with cancer. I lie in bed awake, not able to get to sleep, as there is one thing I always put off during my treatments - The final will and testament. Funnily enough, it seems a lot easier to write one of these things while I am healthy.*

*What do you write as a last conversation anyone alive will have with you after your death?*

*For me, the dying is the easy part. Closing my eyes and drifting off to that next place – heaven, rebirth, the after-life … or, if Mum ever found out all the shit I got up to when I was younger – Hell. It's the thought of everyone I leave behind that bothers me. I need to tell everyone that I was fine, that I loved them dearly and for God's sake make sure you serve White Russians at the wake. You see I believe it is very possible and very common for someone to die of a disease healthily, and happy.*

*The physical aspect is only one part that makes up the whole individual that is you or me. The body is just like a rose bush that blooms in one part of the year only to wither away at another. The rose bush itself is healthy all year round, only its appearance changes. The emotional and spiritual body is stronger than the physical. That is why we can endure so much pain and at times overcome odds that seem insurmountable. The illness and death of one body does not specifically mean the death of others.*

*Lying in bed I realise that I have had a great, full and satisfying life. Shorter than some, longer than others. My candle has burnt so very brightly. I have loved my family and friends as passionately as possible, and have in turn received that love back threefold. When my time comes, it is with a contented smile that I will meet this change. But I know that I will feel for those that I leave on the shore.*

*I ask you: Do any of us really ever die if we live on in the memory and experiences of our loved ones? Every special moment and every blossoming bud is shared with each other and is the birth of a memory that will not be subject to disease.*

*In love and friendship we obtain immortality, the cure to cancer.*

I returned to Sydney feeling on top of the world. Within two weeks I moved into my new apartment in Dee Why, and enjoyed a bachelor life most guys only dream of. I decided to use the location to my advantage fitness-wise. To get to work, I would either bicycle or run from Dee Why to the Manly ferry, and then continue on from Circular Quay to my office at Pitt Street located near Town Hall. I started beach running and swimming in the ocean. I also joined the Dee Why Surf Lifesaving Club and booked in for Bronze Medallion training, which would start in January. However, the most eagerly awaited part of my training was going to be my introduction to surfing. Now I have mentioned it on numerous occasions throughout this story, but for emphasis' sake I'll mention it again – I am naturally a large, bulky and hairy guy. I had the perfect coordination skills for a rugby front rower. It took years of martial arts training before I worked out how to kick something without tripping over and landing on my own arse. In addition to all of this, I grew up in the country so the extent of my ocean experience was the annual family summer holidays at Coffs Harbour, and even on a few of these occasions I gave the surf lifesavers some undeserved heart palpitations. Despite all of this, I was determined to learn this elusive sport and achieve the final piece of my "beach bum" image. Anyway, how hard could it be, right? You paddle out into the water, wait for a wave, catch the wave, then stand up … simple. I learned two things in the following weeks of lessons. First, I was crap with no natural ability at anything (I had already known this but it was good affirmation). Second, I was hooked on surfing, as shit as I was. I purchased my first surfboard, a nine-foot, bright red Malibu and started giving the local on-lookers some hilarious scenes. When not training, working or trying to surf, I found myself gravitating to the bar, Deck 23, on Dee Why beach. I had moved to this locality knowing absolutely no one, but in a few weeks I was a member of a very social and self-proclaimed clan dubbed Team Dee Why. For the first time since leaving Dubbo almost ten years ago, I found myself being a part of a community outside of the Army, and fell in love with Sydney's Northern Beaches.

Apart from the love of my new found life, my goal remained the same. I was still practising my Qigong and intended this respite to be short-lived. Christmas 2004 came and I headed up to Tweed Heads to spend the holiday with Dad and his wife, Heather. I had met up with a mate visiting from China and we rented a Ute to cruise up the coast in – so I could take the surfboard along with me. Boxing Day was gearing up to be its usual bloated recovery when we received a very distraught phone call from my sister who was now living in London. Her Christmas Day festivities had been cut short because her husband had walked out on her, claiming that he no longer loved her, not the nicest of Christmas presents, not the nicest of guys. It was decided within the hour that I would be on the next possible flight to London. I flew back to Sydney only vaguely aware that a Tsunami had just ripped through half of Asia killing thousands of people. That Christmas was pretty fucked for a lot of people.

I was supposed to be saving for China, but due to my newly acquired lifestyle and the Deck Bar, money was something I had very little of. Again, the strength of family support was unquestionable. Mum and Gordon paid for the plane ticket, Dad and Heather supplied the money for expenses. Within 48 hours of receiving the distress signal from the UK, the family had me on a rapid response mission. Melissa had been living in London for two years and had often been in touch and acted as surrogate sister for someone very special to me who had also travelled to the UK for a working holiday. As anxious and concerned as I was for my sister, I will admit that an unexpected meeting with Michelle had me anxious as well.

London was not a trip designed for sightseeing. The intent was to support Melissa and bring her home to Australia. She was understandably a mess and I was grateful to be in a position to provide her with support after everything she and the rest of the family had done for me during my trials and tribulations. Michelle was in Slovenia for Christmas and New Year's Eve, and had no idea what had happened or that I was in the UK, so Mel and I had a week together before she returned to the news. She came straight over via the underground and because it was dark, I walked up to meet her. It had been a pretty intense week, and I could not help but feel nervous about seeing Michelle again, so I did what every bloke does when he is confused, distressed, emotional … I went to the pub first and downed a couple of British pints. I had acknowledged many years ago that Michelle held a special place in my heart, but I also understood that our friendship should not be jeopardised because of the tug of my hormones. As mentioned previously, I was a soldier on the move and my track record with relationships had not been good. I knew that. So did Michelle, so I had all but accepted that this was a forbidden love that would never go further than friendship, if that was all I was able to have with her, and then

I would take it. Strangely enough the Angel-Whisperer had sensed a connection between us and was never comfortable when Michelle was around – women's intuition or psychic? I'll let you decide…

The three of us had a take-away dinner of Indian (when in England, do as the English do), and settled in to a couple of bottles of wine. Mel actually smiled a few times and the mood was lifted. After Mel went to bed, Michelle and I stayed up to chat and, assisted by the wine and a long time apart, we finally admitted our feelings for each other. In true Michelle honesty, she claimed that my experience with cancer had made me a much nicer person – for that reason alone I would be forever grateful to this disease.

Michelle still had six months remaining on her UK work visa and was in the process of applying for an extension. She was not quite ready to return to Australia, and she had planned to move on to Canada, possibly for up to 24 months. We agreed that as painful as it was to separate after finally being united, we would attempt the dreaded long-term relationship, until either she came back to Australia or I packed up my things and met her in the UK or Canada.

In the space of a few hours I had gone from an intended journey of seclusion in the Orient, to being in a full-blown relationship with a possible European destination. Furthermore, my beloved bachelorhood on the beach had potentially been jeopardised by domestication and commitment. This soldier had definitely moved into unfamiliar territory. The bachelor pad was already on shaky ground as I had suggested that Mel stay with me in Dee Why until she got herself sorted out back in Australia. I realised that my experiences over the last few years had taught me to accept the chaos of life. Things could shift so quickly and dramatically that all I could do was hold on and enjoy the ride. China was going to have to wait, possibly indefinitely.

I returned to Dee Why with summer in full swing. My surfing was not improving but that didn't stop me from trying, and at least I was learning how to act like a surfer. I would hang out with Team Dee Why at the Deck Bar or the Seachange Cafe and comment on the swell size, the effect the sand bank was having on the break and how the guy we were watching had just "done a mad pig-dog into a right-hand barrel off the point". Everyone knew I was talking shit and had nothing to back up this jargon, in truth I was still learning to stand up. But they let it go and I appreciated their acceptance. Mel moved in and life returned to some normality (if you can call living with your sister again after nearly 10 years normality...) It was hard being in Australia and having Michelle in England, but I took this as another lesson in patience and tried to continue to save with the intent that I would be leaving sometime in the year.

Within a few months Michelle told me that she would be returning home around July. We still intended to pack up our bags and travel but this would wait as we would work and save in Sydney first. As Mum had been born in Wales, I was eligible for UK citizenship. This was great news as it meant I could travel, live and work anywhere in Europe regardless of my age. Our destination options opened up immensely. I had a lot going on now as my days were focused on Qigong and surfing, and waiting for Michelle to return. I was hoping that Michelle would accompany me to China as I still dreamt of returning to Wudang. However, the journey was never going to be as I had previously expected it.

I was working in a support role for our counter-terrorist response plan. I was performing the role but my mind was already overseas. My career had taken a fair hit with the onset of cancer and it was now travelling in a direction I had not intended (primarily supporting roles as opposed to operational). Regardless of how active and fit I had become since the fight with cancer, I was still not up to the appropriate standard to apply for Special Forces and my time away from a regiment saw my war-fighting capability diminish. I was looking forward to possibly leaving the Army, but I was also disappointed about failing to reach a major lifetime ambition – to deploy overseas on operations with the Australian Army.

My surfing began to meld in with the Qigong. It was me-time where I could withdraw from work, relationships and health, and just be. I was then and still am a great believer in meditation. But not so much in some mystical form that aspires for inter-planar travel. Instead I believe meditation to be any activity that engrosses my whole consciousness, in a way that calms and nourishes. Meditation can be achieved walking, swimming, golfing, bongo drumming or sitting still. It is a time when there are no expectations of myself. Along Dee Why and surrounding beaches, I was able to be utterly me. My mind was so focused on the heaving swell, duck-diving under a frothing white-wash, assessing the right position for a pick-up and being constantly humbled by the ocean, that I had no space to be concerned about cancer, work pressures or travel plans. And when there were no waves, I could just enjoy that unique sensation when floating on the ocean and breathing in that salty air. Surfing replaced China, it became the place that gave me peace. When I speak to people about dealing with cancer or any other hardship they may be enduring, I ask them what release they have. What nourishes them? Those that don't have an answer are usually the ones that are not coping as well, as are the ones that don't have time to do their beloved activity. What could be more important than giving yourself time to heal?

Michelle came home and we settled into a normal relationship. I tried to get her into the surfing scene but it wasn't her thing. As much as we tried to plan for our travels overseas, my constant check-ups seemed to always get in the way. We were still monitoring the residual tumours in my lungs and abdomen. Every now and then they showed signs of growth, but nothing too significant. The question constantly lurked during appointments with my specialists:

– "When should we go back in?"
– "Do we need to go back in?"
– "Do I, or don't I have cancer?"

One of the most confusing aspects of this conundrum was my health and fitness. On the outside I was fitter and stronger than most. On the inside my body was as fragile as a china shop (none of the doctors quite liked going back in there to have a look around in case they knocked something over). I repeatedly referred to myself as the "healthiest sick person in the world". The Defence Force has an excellent medical plan that gives full coverage to members. If I left the Army to travel around the world I would be walking away from arguably the best medical insurance policy in the country. As carefree as I felt when surfing, and as much as I dreamt of spending the next few years travelling across the globe, I could not ignore the simple fact that I had baggage that would follow me wherever I went. This baggage is a hard thing for cancer patients to carry, especially the independent ones.

In late 2005 I took extended leave from the Army. This amounted to about nine months and I was going to spend this time transitioning out of the services and preparing for overseas travel. I created my own security and risk consultancy company and had some contracts ready to roll straight away. These jobs varied from traditional security and personal protection tasks, to airport security training, risk assessments and even bio-security assessments and accessing control planning for a primary industry project. I had no intention of returning to the Army full time and was intent on setting the world on fire with my soldier-styled corporate skills. It only took me a few months before the reality of self-employment reeled my aspirations in a little.

The following April (2006) brought with it the Australian military's most revered day – ANZAC Day. I had a huge identity crisis as I wanted to commemorate this day as a soldier, not a civilian. Although I was technically still in the Army, I was reminded that I was transitioning out of a very familiar and much-loved military family. I was not even a veteran who had served his country overseas. It amazes me how fixated we can get on how our chosen career defines us as people. The daily exposure in a professional culture changes us and moulds us without our realising it. Before we know it we find it hard to converse and socialise with people from cultures not similar to our own. When we are sick or injured, instead of being concerned for our health, we can easily be distracted by how this will affect our identity. I thought that I had resolved all of this in China. Apparently not.

It was a combination of realising the civilian security industry was not for me, as well as missing the Army that saw me finish up my leave and put my uniform back on. I was honestly relieved that I had not left the Army completely as it dawned on me I still had a lot of unfinished business there. I had taken a walk on the other side of the fence only to look back and see that I was simply a soldier, or maybe a simple soldier. Either way, the uniform still fitted me, with or without cancer.

As usual, a pressing concern was the activity of my tumours. Dr Rather-be-Fishing was still thinking that we should go in and remove them. Dr Chocolate-Love thought we should leave them. Doc Rabbit saw both sides of the argument. I asked Dr Rather-Be-Fishing to start preparations for the next operation. After all - the decision was, and always had been only mine to make, a privilege and responsibility we often forget as patients. Unless you are a doctor, chances are you will have absolutely no idea what is being said to you when a specialist tells you that you are suffering from cancer, or any other disease. If treatment goes well, it is you the patient who has to deal with recovery, if it goes badly, it is you who has to deal with the consequences and still make the most of life. Either way this is your bag to carry, so you might as well start by taking responsibility and command of the situation.

Recently I was watching an episode of the TV series RPA. In it, a young lad of about 17 was going through a pretty rough fight with cancer. Like me he had gone through chemo and several operations, and unfortunately was now dealing with the fact that he was going to have to have his arm amputated. The problem was that he had his school formal coming up in a few months and he wanted to look "normal" for it. The doctors began to get quite agitated and concerned because he wouldn't allow the surgery to happen before the formal. This young lad stuck to his guns and insisted in waiting until after the event. He even underwent further chemo treatment to ensure the cancer did not spread in the interim. To me, this was the right decision. This young man took control and responsibility for his situation. He knew the risks, but also knew what was important to him. The surgeons, understandably, wanted to remove the risk, but he had to live with the consequences. For my part, I wanted these tumors to be out of me. I wanted to be free from the weight of the disease that was still slung over my shoulders. Simultaneously, I had a really bad feeling about the operation. Now I am generally a positive guy and I don't like allowing negative thoughts to be any more than cautious reminders during my decision-making process. But in this instance, I could not help but feel a sense of dread. I knew the operation was going to become a reality sooner or later, and I had already resolved to undergo the operation sooner. But I couldn't shake the feeling that the outcome of this operation would not turn out well for me.

Michelle and I were in the car one day discussing the upcoming operation when I voiced these concerns, and suddenly without intending to, I found myself reversing the decision I had made earlier. I had back-tracked but knew it was the right decision. I rang Dr Rather-be-Fishing and asked him to cease preparations. I was going to wait, and watch a little longer – "Sorry guys, false start."

With that minor dilemma resolved, it was time for me to sort something else out that had been on my mind for a while. I was back in uniform and working in the Army's Land Headquarters at Victoria Barracks in the middle of Sydney. This environment was much more operationally focused than what I had been doing in the previous few years, and with the war on terror now full blown, I was determined to deploy overseas.

I had brought myself back to a medical classification that deemed me operationally deployable. This classification states that a soldier is suitable medically, administratively, dentally, physically and mentally to be sent overseas on active duty. In 2007, the Defence Force was very busy with troops deployed in as many different countries as we were in during World War II. We had forces in Iraq, Afghanistan, East Timor, the Solomon Islands and various other countries in UN peacekeeping roles. Surely there was a war out there somewhere for me…

# THE MEAO

Contrary to popular belief, even being in the Australian Army, it's not that easy to get yourself sent overseas on operations. Unless you are part of a unit that is deploying on a specific task, you can easily be left twiddling your thumbs back in Australia. The situation is slowly changing now, but up until 2005-ish, it was very common to see members who had been in the Defence Force for 15, 20, 25-plus years with no overseas operational experience. There are some people who are comfortable with this, but speaking from experience, for the majority of Army personnel, if there is a conflict going on, we want to be a part of it. We want to go and do our job. This may sound psychotic and macabre, but the best way of understanding our mentality is to perhaps compare us to medical personnel. I am guessing that for the most part, a surgeon does not want to operate on another human being. They would no doubt prefer it if disease and illness did not exist and that there was no requirement for a medical system. But there is. And they don't study and train for all those years just to walk away from an operation that could be potentially fatal to the patient just because it is risky. They are trained to do good and save lives. The Australian soldier is very similar. We have a deep sense of duty and the will to help others. Unfortunately, disease, war and conflict will always exist in the world. It is a natural part of the human condition. Although war is a terrible business, there is something that draws the soldier in us to it, a hope to rectify a wrong.

Within a few months of being back from long service leave I had identified a position as *Aide de Camp* (ADC) to the General in charge of all the Australian forces in the Middle Eastern Area of Operations (MEAO). This included Army, Air Force and Navy. ADC is basically military talk for an Executive Assistant. It would be a great job as it involved moving around the Area of Operation with the General and gaining a strategic perspective on the conflict as a whole. I had attempted to gain a position within a unit that would be performing a more operational task (such as patrols and reconstruction), but the time spent dealing with cancer and sorting my life out afterwards had left me lacking in regimental and operational experience. Beggars cannot be choosers, however, and I was thrilled with anything I could get. This job was a blessing. I was due to start a new position within the Headquarters that actually coordinates all units on operational tasks around the globe the following year. In order to deploy at all I needed permission from this unit as they would be the ones dealing with an empty position while I was away for six months. It seemed that all the stars were aligning in my favour as I was graciously granted permission and I began with preparations for my deployment.

Unfortunately my time in Dee Why was drawing to an end. Michelle and I had decided that as both of us were working in the city (and Sydney commuting was driving us crazy), we would move closer. We set our sights on the lower North Shore as a possible new base. I was determined not to be too far from the beach as I was now standing up on my surf board and this small piece of progress had invigorated my obsession for the waves. We found an apartment in Cremorne and moved in just before Christmas 2006. I was due to deploy around April/May the next year and this gave me plenty of time to settle in to our new place.

Medically, although I was fit and relatively healthy, the Army still wanted me to get another round of scans as well as letters of recommendation from my specialists stating that I was in a healthy enough condition to get shot at. It always seems a little contradictory that we need to be in perfect health and physical condition before we are able to go to war. In truth, more casualties occur through disease, poor health and accidents during deployment than from actual engagements with the enemy. Being in good condition attempts to eliminate as much as possible the chance of an Army losing it's fighting capacity of their personnel from anything other than direct combat (this correlation between deploying to war and battling cancer was not lost on me). Either way, I was now as fit as I was prior to cancer (minus a nut and a kidney and some chunks of lung). There was no way I was going to have those specialists offer anything but an approval.

It was very interesting receiving people's different reaction to the news that I was going to war. My doctors, for instance, were shocked and surprised that after going through all I had with cancer; I now wanted to put myself in harm's way again – willingly. Offering them an explanation wasn't hard, but I'm not sure if they grasped my meaning. Although I now had more experience with cancer than I did with war, I was actually trained for the latter. Cancer was thrust on me with no option or warning, Deploying with the Army was a desire I had set since I was a child. Escaping death from cancer was not going to stop me from living and pursuing other challenges. The doctors all gave me the green light. Michelle and I moved into our apartment in Cremorne and I focused on getting as much surfing in as possible before going to a part of the world that had plenty of sand but no waves.

As I was not deploying with an actual unit (I would be working within the theatre headquarters in Baghdad), I had no idea who I would be working with. I had met the Brigadier General I was going to be working for a few months prior to deployment, but he had arrived in the country several weeks earlier and I was yet to develop a relationship with him. The good thing about the Australian Army is that due to its relatively small size, it doesn't take long to create an extensive network of friends and associates so I was sure that once I arrived, there would be people I knew.

The Defence Force has a chartered air service that moves personnel into the Middle East on a regular basis. This meant that the first part of my trip was relatively normal in the sense that I, along with other troops, boarded a flight in civilian clothing and we could have easily been mistaken for a group of tourists, except for the rigidity of our stride and the not-so holiday demeanors. As I had done over a year earlier, I found myself on another plane looking at one of those nose-cameras, contemplating all these life-altering journeys I constantly seem to find myself on. There were going to be a few stops on the way so I settled in for a long flight into a war-zone.

The first thing that hit me as I stepped off the plane was the heat. We touched down in Kuwait at 0530 and it was already well over 30 degrees. It's standard procedure for the military to pre-deploy troops into an area close to the operations, but not actually involved in the conflict. This is so our forces can acclimatise to weather and routine before beginning the actual tour. Equipment and firearms are also issued as well as briefings on a variety of subjects ranging from threat levels and current operations to a show-and-tell of local arachnids that we might find in our sleeping bags, such as the camel spider, named so because they are known to gnaw into camels (or anything else they find meaty enough). These medium-sized critters don't like direct sunlight much, and if disturbed will run for the nearest shadow i.e. the disturber, and possibly up their legs. They can actually run at an impressive speed, and as usual, are hairy.

Time is also spent being acquainted with our allies (namely the Americans) and their strange habits and cultural idiosyncrasies. As much as we look the same, there are some massive differences between our two societies, and our military forces. Naturally the Australian Army, and heritage, is more closely linked to the British. The US war machine is much more vast and complex and in order to play nicely with each other, we needed to learn their rules. For the most part, Australian forces lived and operated out of US bases so we would tap into their rationing and supply chains. This is not a bad thing as logistically their capacity is massive. On US bases you will find a myriad of recreational facilities (gymnasiums, movie theatres, churches, pools). There are also the likes of McDonald's, KFC and Subway. There is a chain of convenience stores called the PX Store, a military version of Big W that sells anything from clothing and electrical goods to hi-tech attachments for your favourite assault rifle. I even saw a distributor for Harley Davidson Motorcycles who assures customers of delivery to their door, anywhere in the world. The prices were pretty competitive too. Each of these bases creates a mini-America and is usually staffed by ex-patriot employees from countries such as India or the Philippines. These ex-pats work for a minimum wage that would put them below the poverty line in Australia but has them sending a small fortune back to their families in US dollars. Unfortunately many of these ex-pats are the victims of indirect fire, kidnapping and ambushes as the level of protection provided to them is significantly less than that given to government-funded allied personnel.

Within the week I was in the back of a RAAF Hercules aircraft, uncomfortably kitted up with body armour, helmet, weapons and ammo (this is colloquially known as being "bombed up"), and doing circle work above Baghdad international airport as the pilots prepared to land. Landing in Baghdad is not as dangerous now as it was a few years ago. Previously, insurgents, extremists or anti-Western militias would take pot-shots at our planes as they were coming in to land, occasionally scoring a hit that might pass through the fuselage and hit an unsuspecting occupant. I remember looking around the plane and seeing the faces of friends and strangers alike who all had something in common. We were just about to land in a very dangerous part of the world. For some in the plane, this was not their first flight into the war-torn capital. They were maybe on their second tour or returning from Relief Out of Country Leave (ROCL). For others (like myself in the months to come), it was a part of their job to travel around the country or region and therefore they took this flight regularly. For me, at this moment, I was arriving at another life goal. I was throwing myself into a war that has been going on for more than just a few years. This was a war not just about terrorism or counterinsurgency or of disposing of a tyrant and his chemical bombs, its roots could be traced back before World War II and further. It actually had the feel of the ancient tussle between Christian and Islamic states for world dominance, and I was not even religious!

The heat was even more oppressive than in Kuwait as we exited the Hercules. During my whole time in Iraq I don't think I ever got used to the furnace-like heat that would slam into me every time I walked outside (until the autumn came that is). I wasn't quite sure but it looked like the roads out of the airport were all lined with gum trees. The Brigadier was there to meet me and I was informed that they were gum trees that had been imported years ago and were flourishing in the Arab climate. As we drove back to the Australian headquarters I was given a quick tour of my home base for the next six months. I was in Camp Victory – the largest US base in Baghdad. This mini-city housed anywhere from 30,000 to 40,000 allied personnel (depending on troop rotations). It is a massive base that includes the Baghdad International Airport within its perimeter as well as a private zoo. The nucleus of this base is the Al-Faw palace complex, a monstrous and impressive piece of Iraqi architecture that Sadam Hussein had commissioned as a tribute to a decisive battle during the Iraq/Iran war when the Iraqi Army recaptured the Al-Faw peninsula in Southern Iraq near the city of Basrah. It became apparent just how wasteful and egotistical Sadam was as the country's leader. This complex is just one of scores of similar palaces he built during his reign.

Camp Victory had its own suburbs with smaller bases breaking up different unit and force locations. Encompassing the entire base and lining major roads and suburbs were huge concrete slabs called T-walls. These were used as a form of force protection that significantly reduced the spray of shock waves and shrapnel created when a rocket landed inside the perimeter, an almost daily occurrence especially during peak "let's shoot at the infidels" times. The perimeter walls also had gun towers located at regular intervals and these could often be heard erupting with machine gun fire as various locals decided that they needed some target practice or to blow the cobwebs out of their family AK47. Al-Faw palace was surrounded by a huge artificial lake system which Sadam had built ensuring the aesthetic beauty of the palace at the considerable expense of water supply to farmers down river during the construction. Occasionally, rockets would land in the lake, showering anyone nearby in warm smelly water, graciously if you consider the alternative.

I only had a week with the outgoing ADC and underwent a form of on-the-job training before I was underway in my new role arranging meetings, correspondence and various inspections of units throughout the theatre. My boss was very keen to see and be seen by the troops and get real-time knowledge of how our forces were going. So within two weeks of arriving, we were setting off again to inspect all of our unit locations, including those in Afghanistan.

It is a common misconception that the Iraq and Afghanistan wars are similar or linked. In truth the missions and situations within these two countries are extremely different. I found myself gaining an understanding of not one war, but two – tactically, strategically and politically very different wars. Always in the presence of a Commander as astute as mine allowed me be mentored and educated at a strategic level I generally would not have exposure to. My eyes and mind were open to the complexities of being involved in such conflicts and dare I say in some cases, the failings on our part as an allied occupying force. Sun-Tzu stated in the classic Chinese literature – *The Art of War*: "Know your enemy as well as you know yourself". Watching and learning as these wars were being played out by political leaders and generals, I began to understand that in each conflict, we were not dealing with just one enemy, but a multitude. It was difficult to understand one, let alone all of them. Although I have just stated that the situations in Afghanistan and Iraq are different, they did have some similarities. In both countries, the Allied Forces swept through the respective regions and the resisting militaries with some ease. These campaigns were conducted in a fashion we would term "conventional" or "symmetrical" in their warfare principles and is what you would imagine as typical warfare – two forces going head to head (with big bombs and guns), using mainly ground as a determining factor of progress or success. In this form of warfare, the advantage is usually gained with larger numbers, better trained troops or more advanced weaponry and logistical supply lines. For ease of killing, both sides generally know who each other is (by uniforms or what side of the fence they are sitting on). After the initial occupation occurred in both countries, "asymmetric" warfare developed. This meant that the surviving resistance adopted guerrilla or insurgency tactics in order to continue fighting the allies or weaken the new government's control over the country.

I am giving you this very basic and watered down synopsis of two of the most significant conflicts so far this century to explain the path that eventually led me to visualising my disease in a way that suddenly made sense. Any military expert who has just read my "explanation of modern warfare" may now feel considerably dumber for the experience, however. I realised that my cancer had tried to overthrow me as the government of my body. Once I had identified that there was a tangible and opposing force I called in some allies to pound the fuck out of this enemy (chemotherapy and surgical operations). The cancer lost this fight and melted back into the population where detecting it was hard; removing it even harder. I had now been fighting my own counter-insurgency war for five years.

This epiphany helped me to further understand what I had been through and how to deal with this disease. It also gave me an insight into what to expect in the future. I had reached the golden five-year mark.. But the Afghanistan conflict had now been going for roughly the same time, the current situation in Iraq a little less, and neither of them showed signs of ending soon. In fact, even though there was no tangible enemy for us to line up against and blow to smithereens, the situation seemed to be getting more dangerous. This meant that I could no longer afford to believe that I was never going to have to fight cancer again, but it did give me an understanding of what I was fighting.

I was able to experience the situation in Afghanistan much more than in Iraq, mainly because I could interact with the population more. Whereas Baghdad airport was located in the same base as our headquarters in Iraq, the HQ in Afghanistan (located in Kabul), was a 15 minutes' drive from the airport. This meant that we regularly drove through the city for meetings or missions and were able to see the effects of war on this ancient society. The scars of Taliban rule and continual presence were very fresh in the city as well as in the minds of its people. Travelling between locations in both countries was, and remains, the most dangerous time for us. Because we are generally required to use road systems when moving between destinations, the enemy are able to set-up improvised explosive devices (IEDs) along roads and trigger the devices a safe distance away from the ambush site. As opposed to suicide bombers, the enemies who use IEDs can adjust their techniques and get better at their craft rather than only having one run on the field … so to speak. In Kabul, we used armoured 4WDs as our main mode of transport. Unfortunately ambushing and IEDs will evolve almost as quickly as the technology of protection, so even though these vehicles do provide us with some resilience, we are aware that there are bombs out there that can lift up tanks.

Driving through the streets of Kabul and through the surrounding countryside was like travelling back in time. Because of the lack of wood and natural resources in this country, mud houses are still commonplace. Large walls surround many of the homesteads or compounds and donkeys can be seen pulling along the chassis of old utes to save on petrol and maintenance. Electricity is unreliable and only available in some districts so the smoky haze from fires (often fuelled by dried animal and human faeces), mingles with industrial and vehicle pollution to create a heavy, slick and unidentifiably off-putting rank smog that constantly hugs the city, unable to escape due to the surrounding monolithic mountain ranges. Despite all of this there is a mystical charm about Kabul. Located in a basin 1800 metres above sea level, this city is the same one that Alexander the Great marched through before the birth of Christ. There are still battlement remains and war graves from the British-Afghan war in the 1800s. One day we were able to go on a historical tour of the city arranged by one of our HQ Captains, who was so amazed by the city and the country that he spent much of his spare time studying history books related to Kabul and Afghanistan. He had limited knowledge of the area before deploying, but within a few months was the local expert. We took the necessary precautions to maximise our safety and were briefed accordingly before setting out into the city.

Swimming Pool Hill is aptly named because of the Olympic-grade swimming pool on its summit. It was built by the Soviets during the Russian occupation in the 1970s and 1980s. They used it as an altitude training tool for their athletes, diving boards of various heights included. The panoramic view from this hill is extraordinary as it's almost the dead centre of the city. There are also remains of burnt-out hulks of tanks and other armoured vehicles destroyed by either the allies when fighting the Taliban, or the Taliban when fighting the Russians. Our mood sobered when the local kids hanging around us looking for food or water, explained that the pool was drained once the Soviets departed, and the Taliban used it as a substitute execution platform. They would walk women, or anti-Taliban protesters, to the top most diving platform and "entice" them over the edge with sword or bayonet. I caught myself wondering how many lives had been lost at this site of mass murder that now looked so innocent and comically out of place.

We returned to Iraq and visited some troops who were embedded with the British forces in Basrah. At this time, Basrah was a city under siege. The British occupied the palace complex in the city as well as the airport, both of which were subject to rocket attacks almost on the hour. Sustainment convoys and patrols through the city were near impossible and always attacked. An advanced radar system had been established that was able to detect the motion of a rocket once fired and could provide about five seconds warning prior to its explosive return to earth within the complex. These rockets were usually intended to be fired en-masse from the back of a truck and would carpet bomb a large area. They were never meant to be used as an accurate weapon. The insurgents had modified them, however, and had them set up on a star-picket or wood railing. They would then point the rocket in the general direction of intended aim and fire it off. Distance was more of a guess-timation and would depend on how high the rocket was pointing. If the enemy had the ability to adjust their aim over time from the one firing location, these rockets would have become a lot more accurate. However, because there was usually a rapid retort from allied artillery, and because of our surveillance of common firing points, this often resulted in their deaths – so they tended to move around a lot and try different positions.

Accurate or not, these rockets were coming in so fast and often that by sheer saturation alone some of them were finding their mark. As a result, the British were constructing thick concrete slabs above the roofs of the mobile-huts used for accommodation or offices. It was general practice that upon hearing the radar sirens, all personnel would immediately stop what they were doing and lay flat on the ground (in order to take cover). You have a much better chance of survival if a rocket lands close to you if you are lying down because the shrapnel moves outwards and upwards from the blast point. The safety of sleeping quarters was further enhanced as each bay was surrounded by concrete blocks creating a roughly 6 x 2 foot sleeping den. This was covered by a length of pine wood supporting two or three layers of sandbags. Good luck if you suffer from claustrophobia. A direct hit would sit kill the occupant, but a near miss was likely to cause only minor injuries and very sore ears.

With Australian troops in the impact zone, my commander was keen to ensure the troops were protected. We were rocketed so often in the few days we were there that we conducted a briefing with the British general in charge of the base on the ground, ate breakfast, lunch and dinner, and slept and showered on the ground. My predicament was that while the permanent accommodation for troops stationed at this base was hardened by sandbags and concrete, the transit accommodation was still the simple tent and cot set up. The effects of explosive percussion are felt somewhat more when you are only separated from it by canvas and a lightweight sleeping bag.

On the flip side, I always enjoyed visiting Basrah as

the food there was supplied by the British, and was without a doubt, the best food available in any of the areas of operations we passed through. Food is pivotal to morale in war, and the inclusion of real eggs and fresh produce makes a big difference to the mood of the troops. The food provided by the US was plentiful, but there are only so many powered eggs, powdered potatoes and deep fried steaks and cheese a stomach can handle before becoming insubordinate. I shudder to think of the cholesterol levels of US troops after spending 18-24 months on this diet. In defence of the US rationing and logistical system though, I will admit that there are still some ridiculous luxuries that are provided to deployed troops. Baskin Robins was the company contracted to supply "deserts" to these food halls. At both lunch and dinner we had a massive selection of ice-cream, cakes, pies and biscuits.

My deployment in the Middle East coincided with a time in the Iraq War when the situation was getting progressively worse. Insurgents were "obtaining" larger rockets, possibly from certain neighbouring countries, and the IEDs used were becoming increasingly complex and advanced. The evolution of this conflict drove a rapid adaptation of tactics and equipment used by both sides. Initially the US used the HumVee for primary mobility and troop transport. As a result the insurgents created IEDs that would penetrate the chassis and kill or maim the occupants. So the US decided to put armour plating on their vehicles. The insurgents put more explosives in the IEDs. The US then started replacing the HumVees with heavier armoured vehicles. The insurgents built IEDs that had a shaped charge that penetrated the thicker armour. At the peak of this tail-chasing, some heavy US battle tanks were being literally lifted into the air by IEDs consisting of heaped artillery shells and anti-tank mines buried under the road.

General Patreaus (US commander of all forces in Iraq at that time), decided to launch a surge offensive, that was intended to regain the initiative from the increasingly strengthening insurgent force. The aim was to saturate the ground with so many US troops, that the insurgents would be unable to perform any operations against the allies or the Iraqi government. It would hopefully throw the enemy off balance and allow the Iraqi government to gain control of key districts that were becoming safe havens for the insurgents. At the beginning it did not seem like the plan would work. Engagements with the enemy increased, as did coalition casualties. It however became apparent that this was due to insurgent frustration and a backlash from the increased dominance of our forces. On one occasion during this time and 30 minutes after I had flown out of Baghdad (on R&R), and an hour before the lunch-time rush, Camp Victory was subject to a bombardment consisting of 240 millimetre rockets, one of which landed along the very path we take to the food hall. Several US personnel were killed and a dozen or so injured. To date, we had been subjected mainly to 60 millimetre or 120 millimetre rockets. Such was the increasing threat of the enemy during the initial stages of the surge offensive.

Included in our six-month deployment tour was a two-week break (otherwise known as R&R or ROCL). Considering war is a seven day a week job with some intense hours, this break could not come around quickly enough for us. It is one of the most talked-about activities of the entire deployment.

"Where are you going for ROCL?", "What are your

dates for ROCL?", "Only eight weeks, four days and sixteen hours before I am on ROCL", "How was your ROCL?".

The Defence Force flies its troops back to Australia, but the option exists to go somewhere else. We are given a plane flight to certain other destinations that are usually the equivalent to the distance we would travel home (and yes, these are return tickets requiring us to come back to the job). Michelle and I had decided to travel to Italy and I had given Michelle the decadent job of planning a mega-holiday. We were going to go all out on this trip. We didn't have a mortgage or kids, and when on operations in the Middle East I was on tax-free pay. As great as it sounds to be given a break like this, it is actually quite difficult to adjust from war to holiday back to war in a two-week period. I went from rockets, Burkhas and body armour to a summers day in Rome in the space of 24 hours. I had to keep explaining to Michelle that I was not perving, just shocked to see so many scantily clad European ladies…

It may have been coincidence but one day, while walking through Rome, we climbed to the top of the Castel Sant'Angelo and looked over the city. My eyes were drawn to the Vatican and the throngs of people lined up to visit the HQ of Christianity. It occurred to me that I had just been in the heartland of Islam and at the front line of the modern day crusade. I have never been religious and I found it ironic that my life was taking me to so many spiritual centres (Wudang included). Having seen and experienced war I suddenly felt very angry towards these "religions" that have caused so much suffering and strife throughout history. How can a belief that preaches spiritual well-being, love and compassion (both the Koran and the Bible speak of these qualities), at the same time be at ease attempting to wipe each other out. Although I acknowledge that religion can do good within a community I cannot ignore what it does at the wider level. I realised that I did not want to be in a situation where I would have to kill or maim or cause pain similar to what I have had to endure through my disease, especially over a religious argument I had no care for. So now I was stuck with a conundrum – "How can I be a soldier and do good, while not wanting to hurt those that do bad, and what is the definition of bad when those performing it believe they are doing good?".

After spending my 32nd birthday on the Island of Capri, I packed my bags and headed back to the sandpit, leaving Michelle to fly back to Sydney on her own (unless you include all the Italian leather shoes and handbags she had bought). It was hard saying goodbye but it is important for a soldier to be able to push thoughts of home and your loved ones out of your mind once back on operations. Family and friends are essential support structures while someone is away in a war-zone, just like they are when fighting cancer, but it is important not to let homesickness distract you from the job at hand. I was now constantly aware of the similarities between fighting a life-threatening disease and fighting in a war zone. I, as the commander, was focused on the job at hand; being aware, staying safe, completing the mission and managing troops. There is an adrenaline rush and a simplicity of life found in both fights that consumes the consciousness and hardens the resolve. But for the family and friends at home it's a different story. Michelle would have to go back to a familiar home without a familiar presence, to a Sydney recovering from winter. She would have to deal with all the little stresses in life on her own, and all the while constantly worrying about how

I was going at the front line. Mum, Dad and Melissa had it no easier, waiting for a letter or a phone call and watching the news. The ambience of war and the group-think mentality I was surrounded by did a good job of pushing the pacifist thoughts I experienced in Italy to the back of my mind. I had a job to do.

Within a week or two of my return we suffered a spate of casualties in Afghanistan. The deaths resulting from these casualties were felt deeply throughout the theatre and ended a nervous run of good luck that had seen us without a fatality for more than 12 months. Back home, Michelle was answering questions from family and friends unaware of my location or well-being. Not that it was ever far from our mind, but the reality of our situation was further drummed into our thoughts by these events. My perception of life took a turn towards a more fatalistic view. Whereas years ago when adopting an alternative lifestyle I struggled with the idea that there is a deeper meaning to our lives and that there is a destiny in us all to seek out. I found myself more easily accepting that bad things just happen regardless if you go to church or have a vigilant guardian angel. I was reminded of Todd's brother years prior and how death can come just as easily to a healthy and vibrant person as life can continue for a deathly sick person. Life is definitely what we make of it while we have a hold on it, because the time will come for all of us, before we know it, when we won't get the choice of life or death.

My experiences in the Middle East were having a profound impact on my psyche. My time spent dealing with cancer and death on the inside was being confronted by my time at war and dealing with the threat of death from an exterior force. Apart from all the introspective garble banging around in my head, I was still having an amazing and enjoyable experience (as much as one can "enjoy" having rockets and bullets thrown at them). This is what I had wanted to do my whole life and whether I agreed with the political or spiritual origins of the conflict, I was resolute in the belief that the work I did was for the good of our troops. In particular I enjoyed getting out and seeing parts of whichever city or country we were in. We traveled weekly to the "Green Zone" (central Baghdad where the US and Australian Embassies were located as well as other administrative buildings). Transport was either by Blackhawk helicopter or Rhino bus. This bus is exactly like a vehicle from a *Mad Max* movie; it's an American school bus with armour. We would hurtle down what was once tagged the most mined road in the world – Route Irish, in a convoy for the 40 minutes between Camp Victory and the Green Zone. Although there are regular checkpoints along this route and for most of the trip the freeway is walled or fenced off, the insurgents are still able to place their IEDs or lay in ambush with RPGs and machine guns.

I had built up a pretty extensive network of contacts throughout the theatre and the coalition force organisation. I also had contacts within the American helicopter-taxi service and VIP jet service that was used to move generals and diplomats across the region rapidly. I had used these guys on a number of occasions to move my boss around, and ensured the pilots and ground staff were always full of Australian chocolate (the yanks went crazy for Tim Tams), and assorted Aussie souvenirs. This form of bribery paid off one day when we were escorting our then Chief of Army through Iraq. Due to some breakdowns and other unforeseen circumstances, the Chief's visit to Basrah was in jeopardy, as was a very important meeting with the British General. Our only option using Australian resources was to divert a Hercules aircraft that was on another task. This was going to have serious knock-on effects to troop and supply movements, which would be felt across the theatre for up to a week. Calling in a few favours from our US mates, I was able to divert one of the VIP jets that was between missions to come and transport our General to Basrah. I had about an hour and was successful with 10 minutes to spare. The diversity of people I had to work with, both Australians and internationals was massive, as was the range of personalities, beliefs and egos. I seemed to get along well and achieve my tasks with the majority of them, which amazed me. These interactions and experiences helped me see that I still had a lot to offer the Army as a staff officer, and although my previous battle with cancer had squashed my plans of being an *uber-soldier*, it had given me some inter-personal skills that were becoming a real asset.

As my tour was drawing to an end, so was the Middle Eastern summer. I had not enjoyed the desert heat and most of my companions could identify me from a distance due to my sweat-soaked uniform. I am a hairy, sweaty bloke from way back, but I often think that the chemo affected my glands, because I don't remember ever sweating as much prior to having treatment. I would easily go through five to eight litres of water a day as well as a few sports drinks. The worst day was when my boss and I were invited to a FOB south of Baghdad for a handing over parade of a Dutch unit whose soldiers who were going home. The day was particularly hot and hit 50 degrees by 1000 hours. We were flying by Blackhawk, escorted by apache gunships, and as much fun as the Blackhawk is to ride in, they are not air-conditioned and the side doors do not usually have windows (for ease of firing out of and escaping in case of a crash). Furthermore, the rearmost right seat actually catches a large amount of back draft from the turbine engines. Sure enough I was stuck in this seat (I always preferred to sit at the edge for better visibility and movement, although if shot at, this was the first place a bullet would go after passing through the doors). For an hour-and-a-half I was stuck in this small, hard seat. We were crammed in like sardines, and I was buffered by strong gusts of engine back draft (feeling very much like an industrial-grade hair drier on the high setting), in a metal object flying over a desert. I was relieved when we finally arrived at our destination, but only momentarily. I discovered the parade (starting in 30 minutes), was naturally being held out on the parade ground – a large open square area of gravel. Seating platforms had been set up for the spectators, but there was no shade or overhead cover for this seating! The parade went for an hour and the midday temperature rose above 55 degrees. We had linked up with some other coalition members and I ended up sitting next to a female British corporal. On the other side of me was a sheik from one of the local Iraqi tribes. He was quite taken by my British companion and spent the majority of the hour-long parade trying to get my permission to talk to her or at least get her email or mobile number. She was a little concerned as she eavesdropped on the conversation, and I made sure that I was well supplied with cold bottled water by her, in exchange for a promise that I would not trade her for some camels. We were given lunch in an air-conditioned food hall where my boss energetically re-told the story from his vantage point, and the fact that I looked like I was sitting under a shower. We then climbed back into the Blackhawks for the return trip. By the time we got back to HQ, we were both dehydrated to an almost dangerous level. I was deliriously attempting to show no signs of heat stress but was relieved to see that my boss was just as stuffed as me.

There seem to be only two seasons in the Middle East, with a few weeks of confusion in between. One day it's hot and oppressive and the next it is starting to feel like a Canberra winter's day. The change is more dramatic in Afghanistan, but there the change is welcomed by all as it marks the end of the traditional fighting season, and insurgent activity reduces dramatically. In Kabul, the crisp air begins to fill with colourful kites that are sailed high above the city by local children. This may seem like a strange thing for me to include but it actually holds a deeper meaning. The Australian HQ in Kabul is located in the same part of town as is described by the main character in the book – *The Kite Runner*. The two adjoining houses that had been converted into our home and HQs were very similar to that of the home where the young boy in the book grew up. We even hired a local employee as a house cleaner and cook who was of Hazara heritage (just like in the book). I was sent this book by my aunt and uncle during my deployment when I was doing some extended time in Kabul. Reading the book had a resounding effect on me, and I was able to feel and live in the story. In this book, the main character reflects on his childhood and his positive memories of flying his kite; kite fighting is a ritual the children of Kabul have taken part in for hundreds of years. Sadly, the introduction of Taliban rule in the country, and the extreme laws proclaimed by the government outlawed the flying of kites, stating that it was un-Muslim. Driving through the streets and seeing these kites now returned to the skies was a statement by the youth that they were recovering from those darker days. A simple sight like this was enough to fortify my belief that the work we were doing in this country was good.

In Iraq, during this hectic change in season, I was able to walk to the food hall for breakfast and dinner without losing three kilograms of water (lunch was still a sauna run). But I had little time to enjoy this relief as I was now busy preparing for departure. Soon my replacement would be arriving and I would leave this war-ravaged country. The Surge Offensive had begun to take effect. There were fewer rocket attacks and the daily battle updates showed a decrease in coalition casualties. It was obvious that the Iraqi people were keen to resolve their issues internally and reduce the presence of international forces in their homeland. It was easy to forget that this was a proud and ancient people who outdated us and the US.

Down south lay the ruins of the city of Ur. It's located on the outer perimeter of a US airbase that housed the Australian battle group. During an inspection of our troops stationed there a few months earlier, I was able to arrange a tour of the ancient city, along with a very close friend of mine who was stationed with the Australian Training team there. The tour was run by the Australian Army Chaplain deployed with the battle group. This was a site of great religious significance as it was the reported birthplace of the prophet Abraham. The Chaplain had therefore taken great interest in the site, submitting motions to have it protected by the UN and educating coalition forces on its history. A Ziggurat is here and is considered to be the oldest man-made building to still be standing, older even than the pyramids of Egypt. Archways and doorways of the ancient city are still standing, providing evidence of fledging human architecture. On the walls are some of the world's oldest legible hieroglyphics. Underneath the city are caverns and tombs of which only about 40 percent have been excavated. Visiting this place reminded me this was a country that has seen war and hardship throughout the ages. I doubted anyone else but the Iraqi people were going to sort out their issues. Walking through the site reminded me of pictures and accounts detailing ANZAC troops in Egypt in WWI and their explorations of the pyramids. History seems to continually repeat itself.

Due to operational security, I was unable to tell Michelle or any of my family the dates and details of my return over the phone. It is easy for insurgents to eavesdrop into phone conversations and without being prudent, service members can say something that could jeopardise missions or transport movements. During our holiday in Italy, I was able to tell Michelle the probable dates of my return. But she wasn't going to know my exact landing day or time until I was over Australian land again. After leaving Iraq or Afghanistan, all Australians are taken to another base within the Middle East for processing and debriefing prior to coming home. Counselling and psychological assessments are conducted to detect any issues that troops may be dealing with. This process is similar to a decompression chamber for divers and gives everyone a chance to slow down and relax before heading home. It can be frustrating after being in a state of heightened senses and extreme workloads to suddenly transit into a slower mode, especially when all you want to do is go home. But it is an important phase after deployment and everyone finds things to do to keep themselves occupied. I spent most of my time at the gym, watching movies or going to the American-service funded café Green Beans to drink remarkably bad coffee and talk shit with mates. Soon enough I was back on a plane and heading home, a lot wiser for my experiences and thankfully in one piece.

# CREMORNE

Although painfully long, the plane ride was your typical flight home from a war-zone. After a brief stop in Darwin, which was frustrating considering that Mum and Gordon were 15 minutes away from me yet I could not see them, I boarded the plane for the final leg of this trip. I was able to make a quick phone call to Michelle letting her know that I would be arriving in Sydney in four hours. It would have been too painful for Mum if I had called her at this time, so I decided to wait until I was settled at home with more time to hear all the news and gossip that Mums tend to store up for phone conversations with their children.

Going through customs took a little longer than I anticipated. Understandably, even though we were deployed on operations as a government force, returning troops are still subject to the same quarantine and customs inspections as everyone else. If for no other reason there may be loose ordinance or controlled military equipment that had been missed during our own inspections and packing processes. The customs officer going through my kit became concerned when he found some utility knives with my battle kit. I had failed to declare these as weapons, considering them more as general tools of my trade. In truth 80 percent of personal equipment, military or otherwise could be used as a weapon, but I thought this was not the time to start up a semantic argument with this guy, especially when he started to threaten me with a $10,000 fine. I eventually convinced him that there was no illegal arms trafficking going and he let me through to an increasingly concerned Michelle, who had been waiting on the other side of the gates for 40 minutes and wondering why every soldier had passed through except hers.

I was home. I had fulfilled one of my lifelong goals and could now stand by the older generation of Australian war veterans on ANZAC day with pride and a sense of camaraderie, and always with humbled appreciation and respect. Wartime had been good to me in a physical sense. No alcohol for six months (not including the two weeks of Italian decadence), and a heavy training program being the only real recreational pastime for my entire deployment, I was in a stronger and fitter state than I could ever remember. Living in that oven of a Middle Eastern summer also helped to sweat away a considerable chunk of the love handles I had developed over the last few years. My time at war had been good for me mentally, and dare I say, spiritually. In a similar way as having cancer five years before, being in the middle of a large-scale conflict had given me a better perspective on life and privilege. Not only did I appreciate my good fortune in still being alive and having the ability to have an active and healthy lifestyle, I was also acutely aware of just how special and unique our lifestyle in Australia is. Pain and suffering are relative to whatever a person has experienced in the past and what may seem monumental and insufferable to some, will seem miniscule to others. While I now listened to Sydney-siders complain about traffic and how stressful their life is because their work mates failed to greet them in the right tone, mentally, I would glance back to the streets of Kabul where a father would celebrate arriving back to his family each day without being blown up or kidnapped, or I would think of the soldiers with artificial limbs and permanent scaring to 90 percent of their bodies having been caught in a vehicle explosion. I also found myself marvelling as I drove through Sydney and noticed for the first time the diversity and peaceful co-habitation of so many cultures. Chinese supermarkets stood alongside Korean restaurants, while in the next suburb Italian cafes served Indian Chai tea beside Lebanese kebab stores. Women in traditional Muslim attire shopped in malls that had specialty swimwear stores. Where in other countries Shiites and Sunnis (Islamic denominations), or Catholics and Protestants cannot live together without committing daily atrocities, in Australia we have Greek Orthodox churches, Islamic Mosques and Buddhist temples all existing in the same street without a bomb going off.

I had decided to only have two weeks respite before going back to work. I was now used to a considerably faster tempo and there was a constant edginess that develops when one is always listening out for incoming rockets, or driving through streets where every yellow taxi is a potential one-way-ticket to finding out if there really is an afterlife. Going back to work would allow me to slow down gradually and ease back into the relaxed lifestyle we take for granted in Australia. My priorities during these two weeks revolved around giving attention to my family as well as to surfing. Surprisingly, my surfing improved dramatically when I returned and I put that down to a better level of fitness as well as a desire built from six months exile. Dee Why was still my preferred break, as I could end the session hanging out along the strip at the Sea Change Café, catching up with the team and basically enjoying life.

Going back to work was a struggle, because my expectations and perceptions had changed. It is not at all unusual for people returning home from a warzone to feel out of place. Veterans from Vietnam felt this especially due to the unpopularity of the war and the rapid transition from intense jungle warfare to a lethargic Australian lifestyle. In many cases, troops tend to either yearn to return to the fight and avoid the hard assimilation or leave the military altogether finding a completely new path in life. For my part, even though I remained in the military, I was in an office-based environment where the majority of people were concerned with the format of an email message or other office politics, which I felt impeded efficiency and support for the troops who were actually fighting. Again, the similarities between what I felt returning to work after recovering from cancer and the emotions I was experiencing now were astounding. I felt like I had travelled this road before, and frustratingly, the ambition of deploying to war, once achieved, now had me confronting the same issues of displacement I faced after wrestling with disease.

One day, while walking through Potts Point (near the HQ I was working in at the time), I passed a restaurant renovation site. A tradesman fired his nail gun into the new door frame two feet from my left flank. Instinctively I crouched into a half turn, back hunched and arms spayed out aggressively. I was unconsciously calculating the options of either flattening myself against the pavement or sliding into the unsuspecting tradie with a flurry of strikes. I stopped in this stance as reality returned and found myself eye-balling the guy who was now stepping back into the building nervously, nail gun harmlessly dropped to one side. My experiences in the Middle East had affected me in ways I did not fully understand. And as I did with cancer, I needed a plan to deal with these changes.

The theme for this book began to take shape during this time. I found that the tools I had developed and used in my fight with cancer were now dusted off and used again. For me, deploying to the Middle East was not nearly as traumatic as my experiences with cancer, but the potential was there, and that was enough to effect a change in me. I had used principles of war fighting to deal with cancer, and as if I were an experienced campaigner and was now using these adapted principles of cancer fighting to deal with the effects of war. As I learned about the counter-insurgency wars being fought out in Iraq and Afghanistan, I saw my own battles with cancer following the same course. The more I spoke to people and relayed my experiences, the more I realised how successful these principles had been in my recovery and my deployment.

Personal change is initiated by stepping outside ones own comfort zone. The larger the step, the greater the potential for change. While a lot of people are happy to stay within their comfort zone, others naturally look for ways of stepping outside it and seek the effects of being challenged. During any lifetime, regardless of whether it is desired or not, the event of going outside our comfort zone can be forced upon us (by involvement in a car accident, a loved one dying, stepping on a land mine or being diagnosed with cancer). I have always been one to actively go outside my zone. I will look for things that challenge me and are a new experience and I believe that where possible, anything should be tried at least once. After all, if I have learned one thing in life, it's that we have no idea how much time we have so it's best not to waste any of it. When cancer came, I was definitely not looking for this type of challenge, but I decided to view it as one all the same. The old adage "That which does not kill me, will only make me stronger" rings true, and I am still looking for the right place on my body to have this tattooed.

Christmas 2007 came around and we headed up to Port Stephens to spend the holiday season with Michelle's family. This is an awesome part of Australia and Michelle's brother Ron and I can hammer the local beaches on surfing raids for hours a day. I had been home for about six weeks and was starting to settle back into daily life. I still did not want to take too long off work though as I now had to save my leave days for an upcoming event. Twelve months before deploying overseas, Michelle and I had become engaged. We had never set a date for our wedding and there was even a moment where eloping in Italy during ROCL was considered (I had been warned against this option both by my mum and

Michelle's mum. As much as I will go out of my comfort zone, I am not suicidal and going against the will of two mothers would have been just that…). We were now ready to take the next step and had locked in a date in May 2008. I was going to take a lengthy break from work and some of this time was intended to be used to start writing.

I had my routine scans and looked forward to catching up with Dr Rather-be-Fishing. Our relationship had developed now to a stage that these appointments were more like a social catch up rather than a serious medical consultation. Again, there were signs that the tumors around the vena cava (the main vein bringing blood back to the heart from the abdominal region and lower parts of the body), had grown, although the blood tests excluded any sign of a return of malignancy. I had been confronted with these results so many times that they no longer stirred up the storm of emotions as they did in the past. The Doc almost ritualistically replayed my options and reconfirmed the complexity of another operation. Still, there was no way of telling if the cancer would ever return, and the tumors were definitely showing no signs of affecting my health or fitness. I acknowledged again that the operation would have to occur sooner or later, but later was the preferred option. I was after all, getting married and the way my life was going, I was not about to jump back into the grinder unless absolutely necessary.

This developing principle of patience and passive watch-and-wait had been learned partly from my boss in the Middle East, and partly from another Australian general that I had been exposed to while overseas who held himself in a traditionally British, gentlemanly manner. He holds on to a theory that "When in doubt, procrastinate" (as quoted by his aide one day), believing that the solution will present itself in good time and rashness is a quality to be avoided. Earlier in life I would have preferred to make a rapid decision and adjust the plan afterwards, a very Napoleonic approach that history has showed was the French general's downfall. I was starting to see the benefit of the use of patience in the decision-making process. The fact that I was already learning this method from my own boss who was very calm and patient when dealing with critical decisions compounded my learning. For a young and enthusiastic captain such as myself, these were wise lessons to learn. Michelle, the Doc and I all agreed that we would defer any thought of the operation for another 12 months.

As with all weddings, the time leading up to this auspicious occasion seemed to speed up. Every weekend was filled with planning, venue reconnaissance, invite list culling etc. As much as I tried to do the manly thing and avoid taking part in the process, Michelle was determined to have me play a role in organising our wedding. One of my major tasks was arranging the honeymoon. This job was not so bad as it is never painful to book a holiday. At the same time we began looking for a place of our own to buy. Life continued at the hectic pace that seems to gain momentum if you let it, but I ensured that time was always made for surfing and Qigong. The Army approved my request for a month's leave over the wedding period beginning a week before the main event. By the time the day came, Michelle and I were both well prepared and even relaxed and because of this, it went beautifully. A few hours prior to "stepping off the line", I was enjoying beers and lunch with my groomsmen, friends and family and I had a quiet moment of reflection. I mulled over the events of the last six years, and with some bemusement, I saw a chaotic, unpredictable and amazing history of events;

2002 – Diagnosed with cancer, chemotherapy, and three operations, one massive.

2003 – Three more serious operations, promotion to captain.

2004 – Three month journey into myself (via China), discovering surfing, emergency trip to the UK.

2005 – Losing bachelorhood but finding love, attempting to leave the Army, learning to stand up on a surfboard.

2006 – Accepting my vocation and returning to the Army, becoming engaged, looking for a war.

2007 – Finding a war and realising I had now been through two.

2008 – Arranging a wedding, surviving a buck's night, discovering husband-hood.

I was looking forward to a quieter life as I felt that this was enough excitement for a lifetime packed into less than a decade. So it was with relief and a sense of contentment that we boarded a plane for Thailand and a relaxing honeymoon. In my bags were some research books and a notepad for a story taking shape in my head.

Our honeymoon was terrific, and as all good things do, came to an end far too quickly. Michelle returned to work immediately but I had a further week off. This book was well into production and I had my first taste of living an amateur author's life. The process of spilling my thoughts and memories into words was broken by a morning and evening surf. This week was utterly enjoyable, and I had made a great start by the time I put my uniform back on. Unfortunately though, due to the intensity and tempo of work, my hopes of continuing with writing quickly vanished. I was consumed with work and any spare time was evenly distributed between surfing and domestic life. I remember during the second half of 2008 having a conversation with Todd while in Canberra (where he was now living with his Welsh wife and adjusting to fatherhood with a baby son), and I confessed that I had never really felt the pressures of life until now. Work was hectic, interest rates were so high it was hard to imagine ever being able to afford to buy a place in Sydney, and no matter how hard I tried, I was still not able to handle a six-foot swell. All this was a distraction though from the real pressure I was feeling inside.

Michelle and I, now that we were married, wanted to start a family. You might recall from a much earlier chapter that due to the size of the tumour in my abdomen, I was subject to a condition known as retro-grade ejaculation. Well this condition had never rectified itself, and as I was unable to produce a sample of sperm before I commenced chemotherapy, I had no idea whether I had any "live bullets" loaded at all! It was time to find out.

Collateral Damage is a term that refers to the unintended casualties inflicted upon the local population during war. A common result of chemotherapy is the collateral damage inflicted upon the reproductive system. In my case, it was very possible that my little soldiers may have very literally been nuked. The retrograde ejaculation meant that I had lost communication with those fellas a few years ago. We were going to have to send in a rescue team to try and get these boys out. I was referring to a specialist who referred to himself as "Dr Sperm" (no need to invent my own witty nickname with this guy).

Dr Sperm claimed to be at the forefront of sperm knowledge and retrieval. He assured me that if there was sperm in me, he's about the best operator available to get them out. He reminded me of a US Marine recon Sergeant-Major with all his self-assuredness and bravado, and was only missing a boisterous "Hu-Ahhh" to complete the picture. At the same time he was a very likable man and I was happy to be under his advice. A number of blood and hormone tests were arranged to determine if I was producing sperm. This was as such as could be done short of a biopsy, and yes, for all you male readers out there – that meant a needle straight into the nut to get the fellas out … uncross your legs once you have recovered from that thought! We also made an appointment for another attempt to retrieve sperm from a urine sample provided after masturbation. I had tried this before in Darwin and knew the process. In the space of 20 minutes I had given myself two chances of depositing sperm in the bladder and, red faced and shaky-handed, passed the vial over to the nurse before making a quick exit.

There was a nervous two week wait while all the results were compiled and we went back to Dr Sperm for the verdict.

For all these years, when I had thought about my chances of having kids, I had prepared myself for both eventualities. But deep down I always thought I would be fine and IVF with my own sperm would be a viable option. Michelle too had held this belief, and so we were cautiously optimistic.

After initial pleasantries were exchanged the Doc got down to business. He explained first the process of a testicle biopsy for sperm retrieval. The harsh truth is that the biopsy had the potential to affect the testicle's ability to produce testosterone. Usually this would not be too much of a problem for men, but considering I was now running on only one cylinder, this became a more significant factor. With this in mind, he continued on with an adapted military analogy;

"Now Matthew, considering you are in the Army I'll put this into Army-talk" – great, I couldn't wait to see where this was heading.

"Tell me, if you were planning an attack on an enemy and you were given a less than 10 percent chance of being successful from your advisors, would you go ahead with the attack?"

"Uh, probably not. Are those my chances with a biopsy?"

"Unfortunately, yes".

And there it was. After all those years of wondering and hoping, it was now evidently clear. I couldn't have kids, WE couldn't have kids.

This was one of those moments where I didn't really have anything, ANYTHING to say. There was a very big lump in my throat and I was not brave enough to look at Michelle. Of all the injuries and wounds sustained from my battle with cancer, this hurt the most.

"There are some amazing advances being made with stem-cell research and the next few years may see the ability to grow sperm. You would be a perfect candidate for this type of procedure." The Doc continued with the consultation understanding that I was processing a lot in my head. He didn't want me to get bogged down in defeat.

I put a smile on my face, nodded, looked interested in these medical advances and gave an assuring smile to Michelle, who was stoically processing the news. But I was not really listening. I can't have kids? The most basic and primal function of our species and I was not functional. Male pride and ego shattered, a phrase was stuck on loop in my head like a scratched record – my line ends with me.

The drive home from the doctor's that day was pretty quiet. My head felt as though an explosion had detonated close by. I was uninjured, but the force of the shockwave that had passed through left me numb and battered, and there was ringing in my ears.

It was only a day or so before that trusted old voice deep in my head brought me back to reality. Reality, in its purest sense, is very simple. It is our mind that makes things complicated. The reality of my situation was that I was still alive – simple. I was also married to an awesome girl who clearly understood our situation and was not going anywhere – simple. And we were definitely not the first couple in history who were not able to have children – simple. The options started flowing into our nightly conversations. Adoption, sperm donated IVF, active interest in god-children and nieces and nephews. Once I got over the shot to my pride, my attitude returned to its usual optimistic outlook. Anyway, we had not yet been married 12 months. We were in no hurry to lose our weekend sleep-ins.

I had decided to undergo another 12-cycle Qigong course during the second half of 2008. This was aimed at detoxing a body that had been exposed to the decadent side of life for too long. I had missed the focus and calmness Qigong provided (due mainly to the distractions of war and marriage). I was enjoying a return to this outlet as can be contested by the body corporate of the block of apartments we were renting in Cremorne. The physicality and specific exercises caused the support beams and walls to shake throughout the whole building and complaints began coming in about this mysterious disturbance occurring approx 1730 every afternoon. Luckily the residents in the body corporate were sympathetic to my excuses and we were not evicted.

I was getting into my training and had discovered the magic of the "kettle bell" – a Russian exercise device that is as effective as it is rudimentary in its task of strengthening and conditioning a body. It consists of swinging a cast iron ball with a handle around, up and down, from side to side. The only thing that could have slowed me down was a gallstone attack. I didn't see this one coming…

Never before had I experienced any issues with my gall bladder, and I was as shocked as I was flattened by this very painful episode. Probably one of the more frustrating things with surviving cancer is the requirement to retell your story to new doctors, or specialists every fucking time something goes wrong! It was good to see that these doctors were being thorough, but surely this shit had nothing to do with a disease I had beaten almost seven years ago … could it?

There was a decent sized gallstone blocking the central bile duct which meant bile was running to my stomach. This is not generally a serious issue and a quick key-hole operation can remove the gall bladder. A reduction in fried fish and chip dinners will usually result in a rapid recovery. Unless, of course, your abdomen has been subjected to major surgery in the past and your insides are as messy as an inner suburb of Baghdad after an American convoy has just passed through.

The doctors were understandably very cautious about going back into that area (like the commander of another American convoy), and I was lucky that the stone passed through after about four days, which ended the need for a rapid insertion with scalpels and spades. The episode brought back some old memories of hospitals and tumours and so an appointment with Dr Rather-be-Fishing was made to discuss this latest occurrence and the old "when should we operate" chestnut. He was concerned more with the spread of the existing disease than he was with the gall bladder. It was evident that the series of tumours, starting from up around my lungs and trailing down the line of my aorta (central artery going down from the heart), were continuing to grow and were going to have to be "confronted" sooner rather than later. This was not good news, but I was not going to look at it as bad either. There was still no immediacy to dealing with this threat and it was not like the cancer had returned. Just the old disease being a nuisance.

I was being subjected to what we term in the military "harassing fire". ( I was being shot at enough to remind me to keep my head down, but the rounds were not landing so close as to put holes in me or stop me doing my thing). Again, I knew this operation probably needed to happen in the next few years, Dr Rather-be-Fishing cautiously agreed, but we still had time – "at any time from here the operation is going to be major. Just don't leave this too late".

Michelle and I had been dealing with this type of scenario for years now. We gave it due concern, but continued to make our own plans for the future. We still had some continents to see and an apartment to buy. Our plan at this stage was to find a place to buy and move into it until the time came for us to travel. We were desperate to get back to Europe for a working holiday, and I was planning to take leave without pay from the Army for 12-24 months while we fulfilled this desire. The operation could probably be done after we got back.

# TWO GREAT WHITES

*"Two wrongs can make a right"*

There is an amazing story about a South African surfer who has an uncanny ability to attract great white pointer sharks (yeah – the really big ones). He has had three different encounters with these killing machines, but one of them stands out as the most amazing, and relevant to this chapter. Encounter one, probably the most uneventful, involved your average-day shark attack where a great white became interested in this guy's surfboard and pretty much used it as a toothpick. Encounter two could be classed as more serious considering the guy he was floating next to was bitten literally seconds after our shark man had just popped up onto a wave. But the third encounter is by far the most ridiculously true story I have heard in a long time.

The above mentioned shark man was having a grand day out in the waves and, being quite an accomplished surfer, had some friends sitting on the beach recording some of his moves on video. During his session he climbed onto a four to five foot right-hander and proceeded to cut up and down the wave, visibly gaining speed and enthusiasm along the way. Suddenly, from underneath his board, exploded a splash of water and a dorsal fin. Our surfer was seen being hurtled into the air, arms and legs flailing around as if he were a rag doll in a tumble dryer. He disappears into the frothing whitewash of the wave and all goes calm again. His mates are obviously dumbstruck and then scared shitless as the magnitude of the incident dawns on them. A few moments later the video shows our surfer running out of the surf (more or less running on top of the water), and sporting a minor laceration to his hand as the only memento of his encounter – that and another toothpick-mistaken surfboard. It is only upon deeper analysis of the video footage that the true story is revealed in unbelievable reality. In slow motion you can see that there was not one, but two separate fins that surfaced during the hit! Two great white sharks, both of considerable size, attacked him at the same time. However, so intent were they on their prey, and so committed to the attack, that these teethy torpedoes ran into each other at the moment of impact, knocking each other senseless and him up and out of the water and out of harm's way. Mr Surfing-Houdini was left to make his way back to shore as the two sharks swam off wondering what the fuck had just happened to their lunch...

So there I was cruising up and down this wave we call life, gaining my own speed along the way. I was happy with life and my lessons learnt from cancer, as well as experiencing operational deployment. Michelle and I eventually found an apartment in Cremorne that we could afford to buy, although "affordability" meant that there were a lot of renovations required. The tempo at work was peaking and I was travelling to and from Canberra almost weekly trying to manage the smooth transition of our HQ. My surfing buddy, Keyring, had just returned from his tour of Afghanistan, which meant weekend mornings were kept busy with us searching the Northern Beaches for a good break. Michelle and I wanted to have the majority of renovations completed before moving into the apartment and this meant coming home from work each day, getting changed and grabbing a quick feed before heading over to our new place to work on it for four or five hours under the light of a lamp. Things were just about complete and we were left with just the painting to do with less than a week before occupation. We called in a few favours and had the weekend organised with friends or family members booked in to "grab a brush" and whiten the walls. Keyring and I went surfing on the Saturday morning, and had a great session before starting on the ceilings. The swell was good and so we decided to do the same thing the following morning. Unfortunately I pulled up very stiff and sore in the lower back and had a very uncomfortable surf. I put this down to all the leaning and bending of the painting. This pain progressed over the following week, but due to our tight timeframe and the removalists arriving that week, I wasn't able to slow down. Even copious amounts of alcohol consumed during my 10-year ADFA reunion in Canberra the following weekend did not stem the pain and discomfort I was feeling through my pelvis and down my right leg.

This brought up dark memories of the past but I was confident that this was just a back condition. It had been almost seven years since my fight with cancer and constant scans and tests had not indicated that my condition would produce anything significant so rapidly. The following week, while I was out of town, I happened to look down at my right leg and noticed with some horror that it was huge. To say it was swollen would be an understatement; it was now quite difficult to discern the knee from the thigh or the calf. My ankle was roughly the size of what my calf usually was, my calf was now the size of what my thigh usually was, and my thigh was … bloody massive. It was no wonder I was having problems walking. I rang Michelle and tried to ease her mind before she saw it, or maybe I was using her as a sounding board to calm myself.

"Hey hon, I'll be home around 9pm. I don't want you to get too worried, but my leg is a little swollen and I think I had better go to the doctor's tomorrow to get it checked out."

"Jesus Matt! That's huge, we're going to the hospital right now," was Michelle's response after she got home that night. My gentle approach didn't fly.

It was late. I was buggered and in a lot of pain. The last thing I wanted was go to some emergency ward and sit around for three or four hours only to be given a Panadol and told to go home (no offence to emergency wards, but from my experience, if you're not bleeding profusely or frothing at the mouth, you just aren't that special). In her very efficient and persistent manner, Michelle made it clear that I was not going to get any peace and rest at home until I went to a hospital. She even threatened to ring my mother if I refused! Mum was still living in Darwin and there was very little she could have done, but the thought of having both ears bashed at the same time was enough to see me hauled off the couch and into the car where Michelle headed for St Vincent's Hospital (where there is a Defence Ward located permanently).

After only two hours and fifty nine minutes, I was seen by the on-duty registrar who was also quite impressed with the size of my leg;

"Something seems to be causing a blockage," I think was his first deduction. I was in a bit of a foul mood so this genius observation was lost on me. After what seemed like a lot of fluffing around, I was given an injection of a blood-thinning agent and sent home – with the strong suggestion to see my doctor the following morning. At least our medical system, if nothing else, is predictable. I was actually happy with this result as I wasn't ready to spend the night in hospital. All I wanted to do was go home and sleep. I had a feeling that the next few days were going to be interesting.

Doctors, waiting rooms, specialist referrals. I was in all too familiar territory but this time my calm and composure was authentic and robust. I wanted to know what was happening inside. I'd then deal with whatever that was found. I was using a classic military reactionary model known as the OODA Loop. This model was developed by a US fighter pilot Colonel John Boyd while he was fighting in the Korean War. OODA stands for Observation, Orientation, Decision and Action. In simple terms it takes you through a natural, unemotional process of collecting data relating to a threat or situation, analysing this data and one's own mental perspective, deciding on a course of action based on your perspective and then acting. One of the keys to this model is being aware that your situation will be constantly changing and new information will be coming in that may require you to adjust or evolve your course of action. If you can get within your opponent's OODA Loop, you can read their intent and course of action and preemptively strike.

An ultra-sound identified a massive blood clot or deep-vein thrombosis (DVT), high in my right leg. This was a new experience as I had never been subject to DVT before, and this explained why I had no idea what was going on. I was the buzz of the Navy Ward at St Vincent's where I had now been admitted, as everyone came to check out the size of my leg. Again, because I was in a hospital with doctors I had never met, I was required to go over my past condition, again and again, and again. I was informed that there are some key factors that may cause DVT – smoking, diabetes, pregnancy, certain medications, cancer … It was possible that I had just been lucky up until now that I had never developed a clot, and today was my unlucky day. Needless to say, the doctors were being thorough and decided to have me undertake EVERY possible scan they could think of, one being a Positron Emission Topography (PET scan). You may recall very early in the book that I had one of these after my chemotherapy in order to ensure that all the malignancy was gone. I was not new to this scan, it was relatively painless, but I didn't like having it.

I had been in hospital for about a week at this stage. Christmas was getting close and Michelle and I had booked plane tickets to Darwin where we planned to spend the festive season with Mum and Gordon and Hector. Doctors and airlines don't like people flying who are prone to DVT, but I already had one so developing another wasn't really the issue anymore – I wanted to get on that plane and spend Christmas in Darwin. Michelle had taken time off work and we were watching a DVD in the room when a throng of doctors came in (I don't have any nicknames for these guys as they came into and out of my room and life so quickly that I cannot remember their names let alone identifiable personalities). They had their serious faces on so I thought it best to press pause on the computer and give them my best "I'm listening intently" face.

"Matthew, the PET scan results are back and have shown a significant hot-spot in one of your existing tumours…" *Hotspot* meaning malignancy – a resurgence of cancer.

"Right, is it local or has it spread?" I'll be arrogant here and state that I was calm and not too fazed, just a bit pissed that I was now facing another fight with this disease.

"It looks like it is localised within a tumour mass." One of the faceless doctors blinked rapidly as he responded to my question. I am sure he was expecting me to be more shaken by the news.

"Right, so this is what caused the blood clot? Do we know what type of cancer it is? Will we need to do chemo or operate? Can all of this wait until I get back from Darwin?" If they were going to come to me with this news, they had better be prepared with the answers. I wanted up to date battle intelligence so I could make the decisions and develop the plan to fight this fucker … again.

"Matthew, you are aware what this means? You have cancer. Do you think you should still be worrying about going to Darwin?" I understand that these doctors were concerned for my wellbeing, but I had this under control. I had actually rehearsed how I would react if this day came and I was prepared. Michelle, too, had been conditioned for this scenario. We were very much like veterans from a war that had just resumed – we were not very happy about the course of events, but I do not know many people who ever have been happy about a war starting up, veterans or otherwise. We were engaged in the war again and had no option but to hook in and fight.

"Doc, I understand what you are saying, but I have had cancer before and I am well aware of the implications. Let's get all the facts laid out and then I'll decide what to do from there."

This may sound very rehearsed, it more or less was. Ever since I had been given the all-clear from my first fight, I had thought about the possibility of the disease returning, I had already dealt with the possibility. Every cancer survivor goes through this in some way or another. In my view, this is not morbid or defeatist. It is the same evolutionary and adaptive mechanism developed and used by our military force after surviving an encounter with a potent and determined enemy force. After you initially shit yourself and recover from the engagement, you look back and analyse the fight, what you did right and wrong and how the enemy reacted to your reactions. And then you make adjustments and changes to your tactics so the next time you run into each other, you hit them harder than before and more decisively. You maintain the initiative and you now have tactics that you can rely on.

There is a very large bite of black humour to this story that I love to retell and it relates to our friend from South

Africa who swims more frequently than he would prefer with great whites. The scans explained that the blood clot was caused by the growing malignant tumour positioned from North to South along my *Vena Cava* (the main vein that brings blood back to the heart from the lower body). Blood clots have a very good propensity to kill someone when they get up to the heart and lungs. A clot in the leg also takes advantage of the fact that as it moves along the body's veins toward the heart, these veins get larger and wider, much like creeks merging into one another and then forming a river that widens as it approaches the sea. Therefore the closer to the heart this clot gets, the easier it travels through the veins. Now my clot was big, bigger than it should have been, and was at the top of my leg which means there should have been nothing stopping it from cruising on up the freeway into my heart. But it had been blocked! Part of the malignant tumour had, over the years, grown alongside and into the vena cava. Down low in my pelvic region, it had actually begun to squeeze and constrict my vein like a python would do to its prey. The blood clot, intent on killing me, was unable to get past the malignant tumour, which was busy building cancerous cells that wanted to kill me. I had come out of this encounter, figuratively speaking, with a cut to my hand, but more than strong and able enough to swim to safety. These two great whites, in their rush to get me, had got in each other's road. And now I knew that both of them were there. I was poised and battle-fit and ready to do something about it.

I was put on blood-thinning injections twice a day and the leg started to reduce in size. I was able to walk (with a decent limp and a bit slower than your average Army boy) and finally talked the doctors into allowing me to travel to

Darwin for Christmas. Most of the hospitals and specialists were closing down for the Christmas break, and it was widely agreed that even though I now had cancer again, we still had a bit of time on our hands to plan our response. The cancer was a slow-growing type that seemed to have just taken up residency in the tumour, as opposed to being a newer and improved version of the old cancer. Next year was going to be a tough fight, so I was more than happy to kick back and relax for a bit before we got to work.

The DVT had affected my mobility, and circulation of blood to the lower body was significantly reduced. This resulted in me not being able to exercise. As the blood thinners took effect, however, things improved and although I couldn't run, by early January I was ecstatic to discover that I could still surf (if you could call what I did in the water surfing). I needed to be in top physical shape if I was going to have a chance of winning this war so I set about surfing once, if not twice a day. You would be forgiven for thinking that this was all a bit of a rouse. How could I be so ill yet be able to surf twice a day? This irony was not lost on me, and I was honest in acknowledging that I was the healthiest sick person in the world, but the seriousness of my situation was not lost on me. As much as I was in the water, I was not able to handle more than three feet of swell. The effort it took me to paddle out behind the break was huge. I would be destroyed simply by the action of walking along the soft sand with my board. I was making the effort to enjoy this freedom of movement while I had it and took advantage of whatever physical activity I could do. I knew things would be getting serious all too soon. I pushed myself to maintain and where possible improve my level of fitness for the upcoming fight, but I was working smart, pacing myself as I saw appropriate. The surfing was making me feel good, the cancer was making me feel bad – I was already winning the fight.

# THE LINE OF DEPARTURE

The line of departure (LD) is an Army term used to describe a point where attacking soldiers "step off" and begin the assault. Up to that moment there has been a hive of activity, ammunition distributed, rehearsals conducted and orders given, equipment checked and units deployed on the battlefield, all in preparation for the bloody ballet that is just about to ensue. Once your forces step off the LD, however, all that preparation is in the past and the physical process of crossing the LD indicates that you have committed your forces to an assault. And regardless of how sound your plan is, or how strong your force, the outcome of your assault can never be assumed, or the result foretold. Having an LD means by default that you are the aggressor. It is the assaulting force that steps off the LD, not the defending force, for they are committed to ground and dug in, defensive positioned prepared, waiting.

I had been more or less assuming a defensive strategy for long enough. As aggressive as I was when I originally fought this cancer, my years of remission seemed to be like an uneasy truce – the cancer being too weak to attack again, me being unwilling or unable to launch a counterattack. But neither of us was happy with the other being around. Most insurgencies occur after a conventional fight, when one force has been convincingly overwhelmed by the other, but not eliminated. The defeated force then goes to ground, melting into the population. My cancer had been sneaking around for years, apparently dormant. It had then attacked a weak spot, but missed in delivering a decisive strike. Now it had exposed itself. This time it was not fear within me but aggressive, determined resolve. I was ready to commit to an attack.

Dr Rather-Be-Fishing met me in his office with his usual grin and energetic handshake. He was honest and blunt in his assessment of the upcoming operation, just the way he knew I liked to be spoken to.

"Matt, this operation is more complex than the last. I won't be the only surgeon working on you. In fact I will only be playing a minor part. Someone will need to organise the different specialists as they are not used to working together. I'll do the organising and get a team together, but this will take a little time. This time there is a very good chance that bad things will happen. I don't mind telling you these things because you are a soldier, and soldiers are supposed to be brave. But I don't know if soldiers are brave or if they are just better trained in delusion…" I had never heard someone put bravery and soldiers in such a context. It was so true and well put that I had no come back. I loved the way this guy spoke, and there was a good degree of truth in what he had just said. I did, however, feel the need to give him confirmation that we soldiers are indeed more brave than delusional.

"We have been happy not to do this operation up until now as it could very well kill you." Nice and blunt.

"Yeah, but what happens now if we don't operate?" Simple question.

"Oh you'll die." Simple answer.

"Then there you have it Doc. I'm ready for this. Michelle and I are well aware of where we stand. I'm sick of putting this off."

This last statement was accurate. Michelle had finished working in January in order for us to spend time with each other before the operation. We had ensured that we went for walks along beaches and through parks and generally enjoyed life to the fullest. We had discussed all the possible outcomes and consequences of the upcoming operation. If things did go bad, I was not going to know anything about it. I would be busy discovering if there was an afterlife. Michelle, on the other hand, was faced with the possibility of being widowed within 12 months of being married.

It is a funny feeling when you realise that each day may be one of your last. Things that seemed complex and of high importance before, suddenly lose potency and everything seems simple. Enjoying the sun on your face or a cool breeze is suddenly the most important part of your day. It is a good way to live and it is a pity that we don't learn this lesson until it is possibly too late to enjoy it. As for possible complications – paraplegia, dialysis etc, these were all put in the "workable but preferred not to have" bag. It is not like I would be the first person to have to deal with such issues. So for us there were two possible outcomes – life or death. Simple.

It was perhaps that my family and friends were also conditioned to dealing with the possibility of my cancer returning, or because Michelle and I were calm about the whole situation, that everyone was supportive and … calm. I have thought since that perhaps there were many a sleepless night spent by them, but I was just not shown that side of their concerns. Either way, the lead up to the operation, and time spent with all the people that mattered to me, was nothing short of perfect.

The day finally came when I got the call-up informing me of the date for the operation –March 5, 2009. Dr Rather-Be-Fishing had pulled together an all-star team of specialist surgeons, anaesthetists and supporting staff. I was asked to make an appointment with a man who would be one of the most essential players in the upcoming engagement – Dr Bow-tie. This gentleman is definitely a personality to be reckoned with and despite his age, is as energetic and upbeat as any surgeon I had yet met. He was not aware of my case and before he would operate on me, Dr Rather-Be-Fishing told me I needed to have an appointment and sell the plan to him. It was kind of like going into an interview, as doctors are by no means obligated to operate on you if they feel it is too great a risk. The term Aggressive Surgeon is common within the medical world, and describes a specialist who is readier than others to cut into someone despite the higher risks. Surgeons nowadays have the added concern of being subjected to deeper and stronger scrutiny in the event of a death on the operating table and the risk of litigation.

I was successful in my recruitment task and walked out with a heavy hitter added to my ranks. Dr Rather-Be-Fishing was visibly relieved as he could think of no other surgeon who equalled this man's ability. The thing about having good people in your team is that they tend to attract other good people.

There was a lot happening on a daily basis now, specialist appointments, tests and scans, more tests and scans, and personal administration that needed to be dealt with, similar to what I needed to do prior to deploying to the Middle East. If everything went well, I would be out of action and in hospital for at least a month followed by an indefinite recovery time at home. The old saying "the only two certainties in life are death and taxes" is true. Unfortunately, the occurrence of the former does not actually see a decline in the latter, so time was spent ensuring financial issues were dealt with in the event of my death (lovely business, but essential). Daily surfing sessions not only served as my required training and conditioning for the op, but also my meditation and release from what was going on at shore. It was much easier for me to handle the issues of the day after I had been for a paddle, followed by a morning heart-starter coffee at my old faithful Dee Why café Sea Change. At the risk of repeating myself – one of the strongest pieces of advice that I can give to anyone who is fighting or recovering from a disease (injury, depression or any other ailment), is that you must find that special activity that gives you a release. You must grant yourself the time to enjoy it regularly. This activity is, in my eyes, just as important, if not more important, than any medication, treatment or procedure that will be undertaken. It is in fact, your medication to yourself.

March 5 was a Thursday. I was to be administered for pre-op and stay the night before in the Royal Prince Alfred Hospital. On Wednesday morning I started with a surf, accompanied by mates Keyring, MT (Mr real estate of the Northern Beaches) and Vinnie. I remember the swell being small but angry, and there were some nice waves to be had, if you could stand battling through a ferocious, shore dumping white-wash. I had done a lot of surfing recently, but as fit as I allowed myself to think I was, it was during my third return through this white-wash where I hit a wall (figuratively speaking). I was unable to paddle out behind the break. Frustrated and angry, I allowed the wash to carry me back to the shore where I watched and waited for the others to finish their session. I was alone, looking out to sea and the realisation of tomorrow's events returned one last time. I didn't want to be in the operating theatre. I wanted to be out there surfing. But I was already unable to enjoy the surfing because of my condition.

"Right, this fucking tumour is coming out, and I'll be back in here by Christmas!" I was talking aloud, but there was no one around. I knew that I was ready and eager for this fight. If ever there was a day for me to "get into it", it was tomorrow.

The boys came back in and we walked up to Dee Why for breakfast, where we were met by a dozen other family and friends who had come along for this momentous occasion. The gathering had a distinctly festive and positive feel about it. This was just the way I wanted to start the day before battle. Tomorrow I would be stepping off the LD and into the assault. My preparation, the planning by my specialists, could not have been done better.

# THE CHAOS AND CONFUSION OF WAR!

Most recounts from veterans of what occurred during a battle are hazy. Apart from the adrenalin, there is a sensory overload occurring that your body and mind have difficulty dealing with. Details and events can get sketchy and you will often hear a soldier referring to himself in the third person, as if they viewed the entire event from somewhere outside their body. The things that can be remembered are simple details, emotions or thoughts. Fear may not be explained as fear but more as an inability to perform actions (battle shock). For soldiers, many of the mind's emotions are withdrawn and broken down into either aggression or confusion, or a combination of both. This is why armies put such an emphasis on drills during training. We break something down into its most basic procedure, and then repeat it over and over in order to lock it into that part of the brain that turns the activity into an instinct and after that, thought has very little part to play. The body and mind simply reacts.

The pain from getting shot or being hit by shrapnel is not instantaneous or specific. Accounts from various wounded soldiers agree that the initial feeling is likened to being hit by a bus travelling very, very fast. It knocks the wind out of you. The body ceases to function the way it should, if at all, and there is a foreboding numbness that lets you know something has happened that is going to hurt like hell … soon.

What I didn't like about the moments preceding the operation was that I was wheeled into the pre-op theatre on a bed. At this stage I was still able to walk. I knew that events might change in the next few hours, but I would have preferred to literally step off the LD and make this walk. But procedures are procedures and hospitals, like militaries, love procedures. Michelle and Mum walked alongside for the first part of this advance. Conversation was not too forthcoming. All I could come up with was to ask what the weather was like outside. *"I wonder what the surf would be like today?"*

I had sweaty palms, not at all different from what I used to get stepping into a ring with some brute during a boxing bout, or while I was driving around the streets of Kabul in an up-armoured SUV. I was determined and focused on the job at hand, with heightened senses and eyes alert, grasping each detail and change in environment. Too soon it was time to say "see you later. Love you heaps" to my wife and mother. I was wheeled around the corner, where I broke down in tears and needed the orderly to hold on for a second before we went in to theatre – 107 kilograms of muscle and I still cry like a little puppy. "Alright Major Carr, dry your eyes and get your shit in one sock – we have a war to fight!"

I was introduced, dry-eyed, to awaiting doctors. Lots of them. One of the anaesthetists was introduced as Dr Pain (spelled Payne?); that was funny. After a few minutes I had forgotten all my worries and I started giggling as the drugs fogged up my head. Apparently the operating room was quite packed when I was wheeled in but I have absolutely no recollection.

This was the second time I had gone in for an operation like this. But what I remember from both is very different, as were the hallucinations during the procedure and through recovery. I remained in an induced coma for almost a week, so I didn't have the chance to wake up and ask how it all went, although funnily enough, I already had an idea of the result from my dreams. The post-operation report is an essay in itself. I had originally intended to include it in this book, however without a medical degree there is a good risk the technical jargon would send you cross-eyed. To give you an idea of the enormity of the procedure, the introduction and conclusion of the report does some justice (with a small amount of my translation);

"*History: This was an extensively planned operation. It was decided to treat the abdominal and lower thoracic (belly and chest) component of his disease, which was the site of the proven malignant dedifferentiation, as the first stage and then in due course would proceed with upper mediastinal mass...* (They were going to start low and work their way up, focusing on the part of the tumour that was proven to be cancerous. Due to the size and complexity of this tumour, they were not exactly planning on getting the whole lot out, just as much as they could while not killing me in the process.)

*"...Although there was probable continuity of the pathology, there appeared to be an area of relative narrowing of the mass in the right lower chest, which would be a potential point of transaction to define the upper limit of this procedure..."* (They were hoping to trace and remove the tumour along the length of my abdomen and then cease before going too far into the chest area.)

*"...In order to clear the abdo-thoracic mass the plan was to include resection of the aorta to which it was intimately related, with a trifurcated graft replacing the major vascular trunks, ie right renal, superior mesenteric and celiac arteries..."* (They were intending to cut into main arteries and, in places, remove parts of these arteries and replace them with artificial grafts. It also meant that there was the potential for serious bleeding.)

*"...The cava was known to be obstructed, presumably by thrombus, and in order to facilitate venous return, the plan was to replace this also..."* (My team was basically lining me up for a complete engine overhaul.)

*"The plan was to perfuse the major visceral arterial trunks with warmed oxygenated blood using ECMO bypass taken from the left arterial to the aortic saddle beyond the point of anticipated lower cross clamp with three side arms perfusing the visceral arteries..."* (In really basic terms, they were going to create a massive bypass system allowing blood to go to the body from the heart, via a machine, while not using any of the major arteries or veins in

my abdomen.)

"*...Perfusing the saddle below the anticipated point of distal aortic cross clamp would hopefully maintain lower limb and spinal cord viability...*" (Subtly saying that it was hoped I would not be left with paraplegia.)

"*...The enormity of this procedure and the associated risk was discussed on a number of occasions previously with Matthew...*" (We were all in no doubt that this was going to be one mother of an operation. If I were briefing soldiers before taking them into a battle of relative significance, I would be saying: "Prepare yourself boys, we are driving into a fucking shit-storm and we may not be driving out the other end".)

The operation began according to plan, my team had encountered a few difficulties and actually commented on the evidence of my previous operation seven years prior. About six hours into the operation, you could say that the only things left in my belly area were a whole heap of latex-gloved hands and some organs carefully shoved to the side.

About midway through the operation my surgical team hit a bit of a snag;

"*...At this point there was unexpectedly high-pressure, high flow bleeding from within the now isolated aortic segment...*" (They encountered serious bleeding, which they always expected to at some point, but the worrying issue was that they could not find the cause of the bleeding. It was like a water main had burst and the flow was so huge that no one could see where the broken pipe was).

When I read through the report I understood little of what was happening. But one paragraph is obvious and this point in the operation makes me proud to know occurred and how it was dealt with;

"...*Aborting the procedure at this point had also been considered but it was felt technically possible to still achieve clearance through the alternative plan. The situation at this point was still quite dire but there was no alternative other than to continue...*" (It is obvious that my team deliberated at this point on cancelling the operation which would have assured me a wake up. But it would have also been a definite death sentence. It would mean that any future operation would be near impossible. I am proud of this moment because it shows my team were confident enough to go forward. Dr Rather-Be-Fishing would have been there knowing I would have kicked his arse if he had let me wake up to the news that they had given up halfway through. My surgical team was aggressive enough to continue the attack for me, and for that I will always be grateful to them. The conclusion of the medical report reads;

"*This was an enormous procedure with massive transfusional requirements due to an incredibly vascularised retrocural / upper abdominal mass, but it proved possible to excise all residual abdominal-thoracic disease to macroscopic completion albeit with dramatic bleeding...*" (We call this Mission Success. I also call this the perfect moment to give thanks to blood donors. During the operation I consumed about 30 litres of blood. The body typically holds about six-seven litres. I'm not sure how much stock we have left after my little escapade so please keep giving!)

My team had worked on me for over 15 hours. I had almost died in that operating theatre and the surgeons were surprised themselves that not only did they succeed in what they wanted to do, but I was going to survive to congratulate them and not kick their arses. Some people think they have a hard time in the office.

While I had been asleep on the operating table, and my

team were up to their elbows in arterial bleeding and tumour excising, my family were doing it just as hard outside the operating room. As experienced as I now am at being operated on, I have no idea how hard it must be as a family member to sit around helplessly for 15 hours, wondering what the hell was going on. My loved ones were unaware of the battle that went on during that Thursday, but by Friday morning the procedure had been explained and everyone was breathing a lot easier. Their personal battles resumed on the Saturday.

There is a term gaining popularity in the counter-insurgency world describing the unintended creation of an enemy or insurgent due to the event of a counter-insurgency war. The term is an *accidental guerrilla*. A good example of an accidental guerrilla is the Afghan fighter who, after being exposed to the Coalition's war against the Taliban becomes involved in the fight because of the death of a loved one from indiscriminate coalition bombing. The accidental guerrilla may not have been the initial enemy, but the threat they create is often just as, if not more, deadly than the original "bad guys".

In all the excitement of discovering my cancer had returned and with blood clots and arterial bleeding thrown into the mix, everyone had completely forgotten about the gall bladder and its little "calculi". The traumatic effect of the operation on the gall bladder was not noticed, or expected, and while everybody relaxed and stood down from Thursday's fire-fight, the gall bladder was festering away angrily. It had turned septic and begun poisoning my system from the inside, unchecked due to attention being paid elsewhere. On Saturday, my family was confronted with the news that my organs were shutting down, my heart was failing and I was rolled back into theatre for emergency surgery.

The hardest thing about the accidental guerrilla is that his emergence is difficult to detect, as are his intentions, capability and location. He appears without pattern or trend, so finding and eliminating the bugger is near impossible before the damage is done.

The surgeons were at a loss as to what was causing my rapidly failing condition. Every hour or so, my family were approached by a sombre-faced doctor updating them on how much closer I was to death. Ironically, they had begun to create their own nicknames for different medical staff and this fellow was quickly dubbed Dr Doom. Nobody looked forward to his visits and updates − "It's not looking good" or "We're losing him…". Michelle was on the phone to Todd who was in Canberra at the shopping mall with his family. Things were at a point where she suggested that he come to Sydney quickly. This might be his last chance to say good-bye to his mate, and her husband. Another of my very close friends − Lowie (aka the Day Walker), was with Michelle, keeping my Army family updated, unfortunately with increasingly bad news. Todd had his wife drive him directly to the airport and he boarded the next available flight with nothing but the clothes on his back. Upon arrival in Sydney he could not contact anyone by phone. All was quiet in communications. He quickly caught a taxi and headed directly to RPA.

I still have amazingly vivid recollections of some of the hallucinations I had whilst in the drug-induced comas (remember this would now be operation number seven). The bigger the operation, the more significant and memorable these hallucinations have been. They always seem to be relevant to the situation, which leads me to believe that although unconscious, your mind still picks up on events occurring in the solid world and integrates them into a hazy dream world.

The day of the operation and the day after, scenes in my cognitive world were very dark. I was in RPA, but not the RPA that exists in Newtown. The ward I was in was like an Intnsive Care Unit, but had very low lighting and everyone spoke in hushed voices. There were few people in this scene, some nurses and passing visits by my family, mainly Mum (who would never come up close to me). I felt like the operation had occurred, but was not over. I would spew up black sludge that the nurses were constantly trying to clean up and I was always apologising for making a mess. One evening, while there were only a few whispering nurses near me, the elevator slightly to the right of my bed and maybe 20 feet away opened with a ping and out stepped an older looking lady carrying a wheeled walking support, which curved up and over her head and had a lamp at its end. The nurses were not too happy to see her and grumbled about her being unwelcome and somewhat bad luck. I had the feeling she was a counsellor or missionary of some sort. She walked around talking to various patients within the darkness in a low voice that I could not understand. I must have been distracted by something because when I next looked around she was standing at the end of my bed. Her face was old and not easily discernable because of the shadows cast over her features from the lamp above her head. She was not scary, but not soothing either. I didn't like looking at her and didn't want to hear what she might have to say. I remember directly addressing her at this stage;

"Excuse me, I don't mean to be rude, but I don't want you here. I have my own beliefs and am dealing with this in my own way. Please leave me alone?" She just stood there, without reply or emotion and just stared.

"Please go away." The demand was feeble, but then she was gone.

This scene pretty much finished after that. It was replaced by another, which seemed to last a much shorter time.

This time I was in an RPA that seemed more recognisable. The walls were whiter, the bed harder and the ceiling had lights. Of all the hallucinations, this was the only one where I remember experiencing pain. This pain was confronting and real, and intolerable. I could breathe, just, but my chest seemed to be ripping open and exploding inwards at the same time. Doctors and nurses, were all around me and I pleaded for them to get me the doctor. "Which one?" There were so many doctors and nurses, and none of them I knew, but I wanted one in particular. "Pain, get me Dr Pain," and she appeared in front of me.

"What is it you want?" The voice was rushed, irritated, like I had interrupted something important with something else equally important. What was the question I had for her again?

"Is euthanasia legal in this state?"

"What?" Confusion, concern, definite attention.

"Euthanasia! I read somewhere that it was now legal in this state."

I knew what I was asking. I still do. I was looking for an escape from that pain. Did I really need to go through all this? It was intolerable. I wanted options, and possibly, some peace.

"No, no it's never been legal here. Why? Why are you asking Matthew?"

There were eyes intent on my answer, looking for a

reason for this question. What was I asking her? What was I thinking!

"No, no reason, I just thought I had heard that it was legal, that's all."

There was a reason why I had asked. It wasn't an option though because my imaginary anesthetist said it was illegal. I resolved to tolerate the pain. But it didn't last for long after that.

The hallucinations didn't stop there, but they did get more fantastical and comical, and it would only succeed in making me look like a complete lunatic if I tried to explain them. Needless to say that it was like my mind was utterly bored and decided to perform a line of complicated pantomimes all centred around an ICU that constantly changed, but was always the same. Those first two scenes have stayed most vivid to me. After finally being able to make sense of the events retold to me, I am confident that I have put these two scenes in their correct sequence, the first occurring during the operation on Thursday and the second, more intense, occurring on the Saturday.

Around the same time that Todd was in the air between Canberra and Sydney and Michelle was being informed by Dr Doom that "You might want to prepare yourself to say goodbye...", an unknown emergency room surgeon discovered a feral gall bladder that was gushing acid into my organs and heart.

I am not religious, but I am spiritual. I would agree these scenes may have been "near-death" experiences (mainly due to the evidence that I almost did die during both those moments), but I do not believe that I encountered angels or had some "out-of-body" experience where I was tempted by the light. Instead I have been able to explain these to the satisfaction of a simple soldier. They seem to be pivotal decisions that I made by myself, within myself. Although it can be said that I slept through the whole thing and left everyone else to do the hard work, I believe these moments to be the times when I had a job to do, and I gritted my teeth and did it.

Todd arrived at the hospital to discover a relieved wife and the news that I was going to pull through. The Day Walker spread the news throughout the Army and a lot of those recipients quietly abused me for causing such a scare, "Typical Carr – always looking for a bit of attention" (quote provided by Morrie).

I came out of the coma the following Wednesday. I had been receiving tunes via iPod that my sister Melissa, and Michelle routinely swapped, recharged and DJ'd. So I had a lot of Leonard Cohen, Gabriella Chilmi, Jack Johnson, Sting and some Tibetan Monks chanting me through the initial days of unconsciousness. The hardest part of the initial wake-up and recovery is not the pain (those drugs are gifts that just keep on giving), but trying to decipher fact from hallucination. Many things that I believed to be true simply were not. To complicate matters, my family usually had to have the same conversation each time they saw me as I had forgotten what was said the last time. The first real questions I remember were from the on duty nurse asking me some routine questions;

"Matthew, Can you hear me?" Yep, gotcha big fella (oops, that is a female I'm talking to...)

"Matthew, do you know where you are?" What am I stupid? I'm in the RPA – been here the whole time sister....

"Matthew, do you know what date it is?" Now that's not a fair question! How the fuck would I know? Give me a hint.

"Do you know what month it is?" Actually I'm drawing a blank, another hint.

"How about the year?" Alright this is getting silly…hang on…..last year was 2008.

The nurse ended up telling me the day and date. I remember repeating those details in my head and getting visiting family members to test me. I wasn't going to get caught out again. That is how I started my recovery, repeating the date so nurses would be impressed the next time they asked.

# THE FIGHT THROUGH

After the initial assault has occurred, and after we have achieved a Break-In into the enemy's Main Defensive Position, we progress into a phase of the attack called the Fight Through. This is when it's very much an "up and close" and personal battle, face-to-face with the enemy, and is usually done crawling on your guts and going from one fox-hole or pit to another, shooting, bayoneting, punching, scratching and biting your way through all the enemy locations until you are clear at the other end. This part of the fight, more than any other part, is dependent on aggression, determination and toughness. There is no longer any advantage to be had from superior weapon systems or specialist teams or technology and it could be argued that this is the most confronting and personal part of the attack, whatever appears one to ten feet in front of you is yours to deal with alone and you have to keep moving forward because there is nowhere to run back to.

The advantage of the Fight Through is that you have forward momentum and the enemy is on the back foot. You have survived the advance through his killing ground and weathered everything he has been able to throw at you, and in return, you have smashed him enough with everything at your disposal to get into his backyard. Just about all the hard work has been done, every soldier now has to hold his nerve and push through the mud and the blood to the clear green fields beyond…

My stay in the ICU ended up lasting about two weeks, although I had no real comprehension of time. My mind was set no more than 10 breaths (feet) ahead and I took every minute as a mark of success. I was anxious at the beginning to know everything, until all the details either confused or scared me, so I learned to relax a little and give my body the time it needed to sort itself out. I was only interested in facts – I was alive. I was hurt bad. I was getting better. The updates on possible outcomes – permanent dialysis, the loss of the use of legs, heavy drug dependency, and threat of post-op infections, all these things went in one ear and out the other. They were interesting to hear about and good to be aware of, but they were not my concern until they became real.

I was always uncomfortable, I use this word because at this time I don't recall actually being in pain. The drugs were effectively blocking out most of it. I was very tired, physically and mentally, and completely incapacitated. Each day however, things got a little clearer and those strange people next to my bed who continually stood with their heads shoved in a freezer down the hallway eventually left (apparently I was hallucinating still at times).

One morning (I knew it was morning because the breakfast cart came around and I could smell the food), some doctors came through on their rounds. I had never met them before, but they seemed to know me quite well and were impressed with my progress (that was probably because I knew what the date was). They mentioned to the nurses and duty doctors that they should try to get me to sit up, possibly put me in a chair, for a few minutes each day and this would start strengthening my chest and lungs again. I was listening intently, even though they rarely spoke directly to me, and I caught on that this would be my next task. I had the date questioning sorted. Besides, sitting up would be easy. This became another lesson in taking it easy. I had no abdominal strength because everything had been cut open. I had also not realised that my chest had been cut open. The nurses eventually got me sitting up in bed. I lasted about five minutes in this position before I was utterly exhausted and my head was lolling around like a three-month-old baby's.

"Small bounds Matt, one pit at a time…"

I was moved into an independent room within the ICU (the quarantine room, which at that stage was not being used – luckily the operation was pre-Swine Flu), which had a TV. This was a God-send as I was unable to sleep for about a week and you would be surprised how enjoyable re-runs of the *Brady Bunch* can be at 3 o'clock in the morning when you have nothing else in life but time and a mind that had become bored of hallucinating. My body clock had been totally fried due to the induced coma, as well as being in an ICU that has no windows, and lights switched on 24 hours. The challenge remained getting my mind to comprehend what my body had just been through. Remember that in my conscious mind, it had only been a few days since I was last surfing and larger than life. Now, I was unable to sit up without the help of two nurses.

Breathing was hard too, really hard. I could only manage short rapid breaths and in the rare moments that I did manage to doze off, it would only be short relief before I would awake with a start, suffocating and grasping for air. I would notice some of my doctors walk straight past my room, look in, and then continue on searching for me elsewhere. This was a result of the massive physical change that had occurred. I was admitted into the hospital weighing about 107 kgs. There was a lot of body hair in that weight, but not a lot of fat. By the time I left the ICU, and was wheeled into the general ward, I weighed under 87 kgs and was so unrecognisable to myself that I avoided the mirror as much as possible. I didn't need that frail gaunt man looking at me. I was too busy being strong.

I had my mind set on progress, one painful minute at a time. In the ICU there had been an unending routine of scans, X-rays, removal and replacements of canulars and drainage pipes. I had a nasal drain that was removing bile and fluid from my belly, that would regularly rub against my tonsils and make me vomit bright yellow or green fluid – not enjoyable when your chest and stomach are stapled together. I had a drainage tube coming out of each side of my chest (just below the nipples) and another coming out of the belly. Unfortunately one of the scans detected a build up of fluid behind my liver that had the potential to turn septic. So one day they wheeled me up and while under some "drowsy drugs", put another tube into me, through and behind the liver – that hurt. I also had the old faithful catheter. There were more apparatus inserted or plugged into me while I was moving in and out of unconsciousness, but I don't have too much recollection of those. I was subject to blood tests, blood cultures and blood thinning injections daily – the rate they were going I would soon require another transfusion!

Without doubt the most traumatic experience during this time was when it was decided to put a "feed-tube" up my nose, down past my belly and into my large intestine. I was losing too much weight, but my system was not yet ready to accept fluids or foods other than through an Intra-Venous drip. The doctors had decided to pump something resembling chocolate milkshake straight into my intestines bypassing the need for digestion. The good thing about this was going to be the removal of the nasal drain. The bad news was that they insert this new pipe up into your nose and all the way down, while you are awake.

In order to get this tube in the right area, it is preceded by a tracer wire so they can see where they are going under X-ray. Either the doctor was having a bad day, or because of a nose broken a few times in the past and a gut system still trying to sort itself out, or a combination of both, this wire and tube just wasn't listening to orders. For two hours I lay prone with a constant scratching and rubbing along my tonsils and rear throat, vomiting and then dry-retching and subsequently drowning in that vomit and biting on the suction tube that was wedged into my mouth, trying to remove said vomit and fluid. The ICU nurse who had taken me to this procedure was my lifeline, holding my hand and suctioning the bile from my mouth. Furthermore I had to lie on my hands, so I was not tempted to grab and throttle the doctor trying to do the insertion. As I mentioned much earlier, I have never been subjected to torture in my time in the military although I am aware of some of the methods and effects of this gruesome craft – I would be confident in claiming that this procedure would be as effective as some of those methods. Sweating and exhausted, the doctor finished up and claimed that he was going to clean up and go to the pub – HE needed a beer! I was wheeled back to the ICU a broken-spirited man, in desperate need of a cube of ice. That was a tough day.

I was rarely alone during this time. Apart from the nurse who cared for me around the clock, one-on-one, I also had a steady stream of family that had their own roster of visits. Being moved out of the ICU and into the general ward was a big milestone that I had been targeting for a while. It would mean my improvement had progressed to the point where 24-hour care wasn't required. When the day did come, however, I was confronted with the fact that I would be left alone. In just a few short weeks I had become so dependent on other people, and used to having them around, that I needed to relearn the ability and confidence to be on my own.

The feed-tube was dumping more calories in my system than I could have ever been able to do if I lived above a food court. The result? Naturally if stuff is coming in, stuff has to come out. My bowels, like the last time, were going to need a long time to relax after such an invasive operation. I usually had less than three minutes warning before all hell broke loose down below. Unfortunately I still could not walk without assistance, because of weakness, and the numerous drains attached to me. The nurses are flat out on the wards and that meant, for a second time in my life, I became accustomed to the reality of laying or standing in my own shit. I keep retelling this point for a reason. It is a very humbling experience to not even be able to sort out your own toilet requirements. It makes you appreciate the smallest things in life – like being able to wipe your own ass. It also develops a profound amount of respect for the staff who comes to your aid and cleans up the mess. Nurses are the soldiers of our medical system and definitely deserve more pay.

I knew I was on a roll when each day saw another drain or drip removed. The doctors were cautious with my progress. I think they were still amazed that I was alive let alone achieving such a speedy recovery, and no one wanted to do anything that might threaten the position. The way I saw it, my attitude, everyone's attitude, was mine to control. It was the only thing I did have control over. I ensured that everyone who came into my room was always met with a smile and a strong voice. The doctors would keep me updated on possible consequences or side effects I might now suffer (temporarily or permanently). I made sure these too were always met with attentive and positive remarks. I was still alive. Anything after that was a bonus. I began to shape the mood for my release. I was keen to be out of hospital a month after the operation – I like easy to work with figures. At first this was met with skepticism, then consideration. I would push my family to take me for walks outside, first in a wheelchair, then walking with the wheelchair poised three feet behind me. I began walking to the end of the corridor, and then out to the elevators with my entourage following close behind. Soon I was accompanying my visitors down to the hospital café where I would have an apple juice. Every now and then the doctors might see me walking at which point I would straighten my back further and give them a broad smile, a proud smile but a challenging one. These were all good tools in regards to a successful Psy-Ops campaign (psychological warfare). I was warned not to rush the recovery process, and I wasn't, but I was setting a tempo to work to and letting everyone know that I was back, that I was strong.

I was released from hospital one month and one week after the operation that had almost killed me (twice), the same one which had saved my life. I still think the doctors held onto me for that extra seven days just to prove a point. That was fine, the optimist in me said that I could have been stuck in there longer.

I was under no misconception that leaving the hospital meant a full recovery. An operation of this magnitude was probably going to take me 12 months to get over. But it was another one of those short-term goals that constantly filled my vision. I was determined to walk myself out of hospital. I walked the length of the hospital to the discharge desk, then out to the car. Our apartment is on the first floor of the block and those stairs almost finished me … almost.

I walked into my own apartment a month and a week since walking out of it, to the cheers of my family. I slumped on the couch exhausted but smiling and although I had some sleeping tablets, I didn't really need them that night.

It is amazing how a change in surroundings can affect recovery. Michelle nursed me and fed me, and as was now the norm, each day was that little bit better. A month later, two months since the operation, I was able to visit the Sea Change café in Dee Why and gaze out across the ocean. I think I sat in the same spot as I did the day before I went in to hospital. What a fucking moment that was.

As I am writing this chapter, I am about six-and-a-half months into my recovery, and I have just celebrated the fact that I have made it to my 33rd birthday. I have been for a swim where I did 20 laps of the pool (slowly and with breaks) and last week I learned how to Stand Up Paddle board (SUP) – a lead-up activity before attempting the surfboard. I am far from recovered and my heart rate goes ballistic whenever I go up a set of stairs, a hill, or move too quickly. But I am so far from that gaunt and thin man who I was unable to confront in the mirror five months ago that my restrictions don't worry me too much. Recovery is slow, frustratingly so, but that is natural and I only need to read that post-op report to remind myself how lucky I am to have recovered at all.

Maybe one of the most ironic things I am discovering at the moment is the degree of unhappiness everyone around me is experiencing. Dr Bow-tie warned me of the chance that I would experience some form of post-op depression; a common effect after going through traumatic surgery. Instead I find myself happier and more gracious for the simple things that many people I know take for granted. So many people are walking around with the stress of work or some other mundane complaint that I find myself almost thankful that my experiences have shown me a greater appreciation of life, however brief it might be.

From here my forces and I will continue the fight (after a bit of well deserved R&R). Unfortunately the doctors were unable to remove the tumour in its entirety as this would have been as effective as a shot to the head in killing me. Sometime in the future we will most probably go back in for another "stoush". There are a number of smaller tumours in my lungs as is consistent with my disease. My circumstance seems to be that I will find it hard to ever claim complete victory from this particular disease, and providing I maintain a positive and dominating attitude over my situation, even in death this disease will be unable to claim victory over me. Who knows what weapons will be developed in the future that could see the end of this disease altogether, but in the meantime I'll just have to slog it out.

Time is an amazing and confusing phenomenon. When we are healthy and happy, it goes quickly, too quickly and we can easily forget that it is a finite resource. When we are in pain, however, time slows down sadistically. Every small moment is captured and held, and future thoughts of reprieve are difficult to comprehend. But that is just our mind playing tricks on us. Time doesn't speed up or slow down. It is constant. This gives us the chance to hold on to the good times, relish them, while enduring the bad times, knowing they will pass.

My thoughts on being sick have changed through this war of mine. Without the bad times, I would never have appreciated the good times. I cannot imagine what my life would have been without cancer, I no longer try to. I have never seen myself as a victim of the disease but I do consider myself a veteran. My mates will agree that I was never the greatest tactician or the ultimate soldier, but I believe I have fought this war in my own way – perfectly and without regret.

On death, my thoughts are more simple and practical than ever before. Winning a battle with cancer means that I have just avoided that bullet for a little longer. I don't want to gauge a successful life in terms of length, but rather in attitude and appreciation. Cancer hasn't killed me, but it might in the future as might something from left field, like choking on a ham sandwich. But now that I can see how close death has been and is, I'm privileged with the gift of seeing and appreciating life in its fleeting, brief and beautiful moment. If a soldier is shot and killed in battle it does not mean he or she failed at being a soldier, or that we have witnessed a wasted life, because that would not do justice to the life that was lived up to that point. It simply just happened. That soldier hopefully died doing something that they believed in. The beauty of being a true soldier, whether employed in an Army or not, is having the ability to live life each day at a time, knowing that each one could be your last. It is never giving up on the fight to see another sunrise.

# THE PRINCIPLES OF WAR

One of the things I love most about the military is how it can turn any difficult or complex issue into a series of very simple ones. In order to teach complex skills to soldiers as simple and practical as myself, the Army has to break down every component of required skills or knowledge into basic principles, which can then be built upon as the subject becomes more complicated; from there the soldier's ability to comprehend the subject improves. Many military professionals are trained to, and subsequently have, the ability to manage large complicated projects, as they will break the problem down to its most simple components before the planning and execution of solutions. Without realising what was going on, I automatically adopted this style of military appreciation from the moment I was diagnosed with this disease. As I progressed in my career, a deeper understanding of the military thought processes allowed me to refine the management of my disease. Ironically, I believe that my experiences and lessons learned through battling cancer actually led to an improvement of me as an officer, and as a person.

I mentioned earlier in the book the quote "That which does not destroy you, will only make you stronger", and how I am determined to have it tattooed on the bottom of my back (one of the few places on my body that a tattoo would be seen through all the hair). However, there is another quote that is equally true, and so similar in meaning that I get confused as to which one I should actually get: "Those who fail to learn from history are destined to repeat it". I am not a qualified or educated medical practitioner. I would also not be so arrogant to classify myself as a great military leader or war fighter. But I will lay claim to being an expert in both strategising and conducting the close quarter battle with cancer. I have been studious in my application of lessons learned from previous engagements with this aggressive disease, and have ensured that each engagement results in me being stronger and smarter than before. Naturally, I am not physically stronger than I may have been if this war had not been fought. But I have always striven to be as strong (physically and mentally) as possible at any given moment. It's the moment that you let your guard down that a decisive blow can be dealt by the enemy and considering we only have one life, our guard had best not be left down.

When confronted by the very real prospect of death, as you are when diagnosed with a life-threatening disease, or when you find yourself caught in an ambush from a local insurgent force the questioning of life's purpose will inevitably pop up. Soon or sometime in the future when you allow yourself to catch a breath and reflect on what the fuck has just happened. My reflections found no tangible reason why bad, or good, things occur, and so I find there is no point in getting upset or offended when things don't quite go my way (like losing a testicle, or a parking spot at the supermarket). But where I move away from this belief is when I look at the opportunities that an experience can provide us with.

I created, among many other things, a strong purpose to fight for and enjoy this life once I was diagnosed with cancer, to always appreciate every day I have. Another purpose was to write this book, and to outline a possible battle plan that others might use as a template during their own war. Here are some principles for those in need of a bit of direction or are maybe struggling to deal with their situation.

Instead of getting too worked up over the reality that you have suddenly been hurled into a war against a disease or illness or injury or tragedy that you didn't ask for, try accepting the fact that you are now a soldier, a leader, with whole armies of specialists and support structures at your command and disposal. Try accepting that this type of war has been fought before and there are already effective manoeuvres and weapons developed that you can use in your fight. Try accepting that you don't really have a choice and this war is now your reality, get aggressive (at the illness, not at other people…) and see if some of these principles can help you out.

# THE COIN WAR WITH CANCER.

I see the war with cancer as one of a Counter Insurgency (COIN) war. It was not until I deployed to the Middle East and actually understood what a COIN war is that this analogy occurred to me. COIN is a complex war to explain, let alone fight, and that is the reason why the Coalition is having such a hard time in Afghanistan and Iraq. COIN warfare is not new. In fact examples can be found all through history. Afghanistan has been in some stage of a COIN war for hundreds of years, and even Alexander the Great was not able to fully control the region. In most cases, however, an insurgency develops after a decisive and complete defeat of a state has been achieved, followed by an occupation. Guerilla warfare is then adopted by forces of the occupied state aimed at undermining the governance of the occupying force. The Mujihadeen's strategy for destroying the occupying Russian forces was "death by a thousand cuts".

Like it or not, cancer cells originate from us. They are cells that have gone rogue for one reason or another. The disease could be seen as an extremist faction developing from within, an enemy that silently grows in numbers and strength exponentially and outside the body's natural defence force's ability to control. By the time of diagnosis, this disease is usually at a stage where it's causing a civil war within our body. When the doctors tell us that we have malignant tumours, the enemy has advanced enough to have developed its own bases from which to operate (if we are lucky we are then able to target these bases).

Like the military, the medical system uses principles to formalise general, practiced and accepted procedures when dealing with common diseases. One set of principles I have come across when dealing with cancer, which is quite generic is;

1. Investigation
2. Diagnosis
3. Treatment
4. Follow-up/palliative care

A set of principles used by the British military in their COIN doctrine (remembering that over the years the British Empire has had quite a lot of experience in COIN warfare – Ireland, Afghanistan, New Zealand);

1. Identify
2. Isolate
3. Neutralise
4. Negotiate

With a little imagination you can see the similarities. Each military has its own Principles of COIN, but cancer treatment generally follows a similar thread by identifying who the enemy is, followed by attempting to separate the enemy from the general population. The enemy's greatest strength is its ability to hide within the population (our body's organs, lymphatic system, blood). It is almost impossible to attack the enemy without indirectly or directly attacking our own body. This means that collateral damage is inevitable and at the very least we will have a few battle scars as a memento of the war. As big and grotesque as the scars are that dominate my body, I carry them with pride. These scars are a reminder of what was once real, and a reminder that each day is to be appreciated.

Scars are not such a bad thing, especially if it means you are still alive. We will need to accept that collateral damage is going to occur in order to succeed in the third phase – neutralisation/treatment can come in many different forms. Conventional medicine relies heavily on; 1 – Chemotherapy, 2 – Radiotherapy and 3 – Surgery. Or a combination of these. In Army terms I see these three forms of treatment as; 1 – Conventional Forces, 2 – Barrage and 3 – Special Forces Operations.

1. Chemotherapy (Conventional Forces) is a very attritionist approach. It is non-discriminative in its surge through the body, essentially killing and destroying everything it encounters. Malignant cancer cells are regenerating rapidly and consume whatever resource is available, so the cancer draws in the chemo and poisons itself more quickly than normal cells (greedy buggers). The overall intent behind chemo is that whatever substance you pump into your system destroys the cancer cells quicker than it destroys the healthy cells (the good citizens). After the cancer is killed, the body can start cleaning up the debris caused by the ravages of war.

2. Radiotherapy is more like blockading a specific part of the body, and then bombing the shit out of that area with a serious barrage of radio waves. It is used when surgery is difficult or impossible, or when there is a very specific concentration of cancer that can be blasted. Radio waves, like chemo, are very damaging to all cells and so it is hoped

that the body will survive long enough for the cancer to be killed, then the re-building and debris clearing can start. This treatment was never an option for me as my disease had advanced throughout my lymphatic system and therefore was too widely spread for radiotherapy to be effective. From what I have seen from others who have undergone this treatment, the markings that are painted on your body to "aim" the treatment are similar to the targeting system markings you will see by militaries when directing smart bombs.

3. Surgery is our Special Forces (like Commandos or SAS). It involves conducting direct insertions into our body, working in and around vital organs and removing the threat *en bloc*. There is a requirement for combined employment of specialists and technical equipment intent on delicately removing the disease with minimal disturbance to the rest of the body. Surgery can be very tricky as well, mainly because the body doesn't like being cut open.

These treatments are all quite aggressive and invasive and Western in their approach, like the COIN principles. Other treatments, alternative treatments, focus on assisting the body to defeat the cancer on its own. This may include improving the immune system through the use of organic foods, vitamins or nutrients that are known to have an effect on cancerous cells, focusing mental power, increasing ones own energy and directing this energy to clear the disease with good intentions or harnessing the healing properties of particular foods. There are, of course, various energetic therapies that fall within this category which are too numerous to mention in this book.

During my exposure to alternative methods, I discovered

that some of them can be very helpful, and some are absolutely useless. I found no alternative method that could be seen as the ultimate weapon against cancer. Unfortunately many methods and medicines claim to cure cancer but have mysteriously never been available on the commercial market, or have been suspiciously down-played by the medical fraternity. I believe alternative medicines have their place in cooperating with conventional medicine to create a stronger well-rounded fighting force, but believe me when I say that there is, as yet, no easy way out of this fight.

Western medicine is very good at the physical fighting, but not good at helping out with the mental battle that is going on in your head. This is where the alternative methods can best be employed, by providing direction, focus and a positive attitude. Out of all the alternative methods I explored, the two methods that provided the most benefit were, strangely enough, Qigong and surfing. I can already hear some of you reading this and scoffing at how surfing could possibly be classed as an alternative medicine. But how much stranger is my method than someone claiming that I should drink my own piss? Practicing Qigong and floating on fibreglass in the ocean made me feel good. Cancer made me feel bad – to me that counts as medicine. Doing Qigong and surfing emptied my head, while cancer was always filling my head with un-answerable questions. What do you like doing that makes you feel good? Chances are your answer will be your elixir…

# KNOW YOUR ENEMY

Sun Tzu said:

*"Know the enemy and know yourself; in a hundred battles, you will never be defeated. When you are ignorant of the enemy but know yourself, chances of winning or losing are equal. If ignorant both of your enemy and of yourself, you are sure to be defeated in every battle."*

Ironically we rarely stop to discover who we are and what we want in life, and it usually takes a life-threatening ordeal for us to learn about whom we are inside, and sometimes this lesson is learned too late. You are not going to discover who you are or how you are going to defeat a disease by reading a book. You will discover this through your own journey, but there is a lot you can learn about the enemy in the meantime.

Cancer is a generic term used to identify a group of more than 200 diseases all sharing common characteristics. Probably the most common characteristic is the unregulated growth and spread of cells to other parts of the body. All cells within the body have the ability to grow or regenerate. They also have a little switch that stops them from regenerating continuously and uncontrollably. In cancerous cells, the switch is broken for some reason or another and so those particular cells keep regenerating. Additionally, due to the rapidity of their growth, these cells consume huge amounts of fuel, stealing resources from the rest of the body.

The body's immune system is generally geared up to fight these types of cells, and so it could be said that most people have minute amounts of cancerous cells in their body that are kept under control by the body's defences. When the body's immune system is not working correctly, or when the body is exposed to strong external or abnormal elements, these cells can grow un-checked and gain in strength and momentum to a point where the body's defences can no longer control the spread.

If you are a medical moron like me, learning what cancer is can be difficult. Anyone who actually knows tends to explain it in a language that is beyond the comprehension of a simple soldier. I found that it was easier to break down the intelligence I gained regarding my disease into two groups: Exterior-driven Intelligence, and Internally-driven Intelligence. There was what I was told from others (doctors, journals, other autobiographies, etc) and what I was feeling and experiencing myself. These two groups are inter-related and able to be combined to paint a picture of what is going on inside my body. It took a long time to understand what was being said to me about my disease, but it never took long for me to feel the effects.

Doctors can tell you what is going on inside you as much as they like. But at the end of the day, it was me who had to take all that information home and process and deal with it. There is a strong feeling of betrayal when faced with the fact that it is your own body killing you as opposed to a guy wielding an AK-47 and shooting at you from a window. For me, avoiding that feeling of betrayal was achieved by looking at the disease as an external force, something I could grip onto and wrestle. I ensured that I was emotionally separated from my disease. If I accepted that this disease was a part of me, as opposed to being "inside" me, then there was no safe ground for me.

Knowing my enemy meant listening and watching for signs of activity, having regular scans and tests to watch its movements and understanding the explanations from doctors regarding possible enemy intentions and attacks. The disease is supported by forces such as fear, negative emotions, secondary infections, blood-clots and lethargy. All these supporting forces need to be identified and understood, so I can read the patterns of an upcoming battle. As in all wars, some of this information can come in almost too late (but better late than never).

When I was able to know myself, I was able to anticipate and develop my reactions to the disease. I could then prepare for possible outcomes. It meant continually training my body and mind so it could deal with the battle stress that would follow. My advice – learn about the disease you are dealing with, but also spend lots of time learning about yourself.

# AN AUSTRALIAN WAY OF FIGHTING A WAR

I am a professional soldier. I have been in the Army for almost 15 years. Half of those years have been spent fighting cancer. I know the Army successfully trained me as a soldier because, without knowing it, I instinctively used the skills and principles I was taught during training in my own personal war. You don't have to be in the Army however to utilise the principles that I found so effective but you do have to be willing to be a soldier, and a commander. You have to be ready to fight. I was taught the following principles during officer training and thought that I had forgotten them as soon as I went to the pub. The trick to any effective training is repetition. It will not be enough to just read them. They need to be applied and trusted and referred to when times get difficult. If you are anything like me, you won't even realise how useful they are until you get the chance to step back from the front line and reflect on what has happened.

Every military world-wide has its own slant on how to best fight a war, and win it. The principles themselves are not as important as the diligence spent on applying them. I have used ten principles similar to those that the Australian Army highlights as important to war-fighting, and then modified them specifically to the war on cancer. They are guidelines and suggestions that I hope will make someone else's fight that little bit easier.

## 1. Selection and maintenance of the aim

Every strategy needs an aim; a desired end result. This aim needs to be achievable and realistic, and is the life-line that is gripped on to when you are drowning. It is your compass in a foggy battlefield. For a while I believed my aim was to stay alive, but then I asked myself one day whether dying meant that I had lost the war? Had people who died from cancer failed? I decided that dying is not a result of failing. Giving up hope was my bench-mark for failing. My aim is to never stop fighting. This is a simple aim and easily achievable and gives me dignity in the event (an inevitable event) of dying. Once you have found your aim, you can then set up short-term goals to keep you on the right path, achieving the aim will take your life time and it's easy to get distracted. Short term goals can be really, really short – like taking the next breath, or making it through another biopsy. Or they can be mid-term, like getting back on a surf board before Christmas. They are those little gems that you create and can celebrate when achieved. They always do wonders for morale as well as giving you something to look forward to. Having an aim is also a vital key to successful leadership. It's a common outcome in the Army to see all the soldiers in a unit portraying the same qualities as their officer. The term leading by example is used to encourage officers to set the standards that they find critical to soldiering and then personally living up to those standards every day. Soldiers, who are always watchful, take note of these standards, and as respect develops between the unit and the leader, so to do the standards. I found that if I set a strong and focused aim when fighting this disease my family, friends and even medical staff followed suit. This gave me ownership of the aim and attitudes of my team. This strength and determination was contagious, and I was then always surrounded by positive attitudes. By far the best example of this principle was during my last operation when the massive loss of blood became life threatening. The doctors had the option to conclude the operation without achieving their aim. Dr Rather-be-Fishing stated that the only reason they continued with the operation was because he knew my aim and believed in it himself. If I had died during that operation, it was not going to be due to lack of fighting on their part or mine.

## 2. Cooperation

A team is made up of a number of individuals, all working together towards a common goal or aim. Everyone has their job to do in order to achieve the team's aim and helping each other is vital. When planning military campaigns, we are taught that it is better to integrate and synchronise tanks with infantry, supported by artillery and supplied by logistics units. This emphasis on cooperation is called the combined arms approach and such a force will be stronger, and achieve greater results, than if these units were working individually. The team you find yourself surrounded by when diagnosed with cancer is essentially no different. Within the medical units there are oncologists, surgical specialists, general practitioners and nurses; all working from different angles and relying on the cooperation of each other. But your friends, family and social or charity networks are all units that need to be integrated into the team and given direction too. When first diagnosed I felt alone in my fight. I attempted to fight alone, even though I was surrounded by a multitude of friends, family and professionals. Not only did I lack the ability to ask for their help, I also lacked the knowledge of how they could help. Mum started the ball rolling by attending every medical appointment she could. Asking questions I had not thought of, and keeping a diary of specialist appointments. Dad in all his pre-historic glory logged onto the internet and researched the disease, providing me with technical advice that the doctors had explained but I had not heard. Some doctors didn't get along with each other, or with me. The team needed management and to be focused on the aim. This was my job. It would have been impossible for me to fight this disease on my own. Everyone around me became a critical component that provided treatment or support. Most veterans will agree that the most important tool in surviving a battle is having your mates and a good team around you. This is no different.

## 3. Security

Being in a battle is dangerous enough without leaving yourself open to flank or rear attacks. Having good security means keeping your guard up and not leaving yourself vulnerable to attack. In boxing, this would equate to never throwing a punch without leaving the other hand back on guard. When fighting cancer, I found the meaning of security is twofold. The first is to have a safe-base. The battle with this disease is fought in the body as well as the mind. I needed somewhere to go to relax and be safe from the intensity of the battle. I now have Forward Operating Bases (FOBs) all over my life, both physically and mentally so there is always a secure place for me to withdraw if things get a bit too heavy. I have Darwin, Dee Why, Wudang and any stretch of water where I can surf, float or paddle. These places provide me with a sanctuary where I can re-group during the fight.

The other side of security is reducing the disease's ability to surprise me. Security is about knowing what could happen so you can position yourself to deal with those possibilities. When cancer returned the second time it did not crush me, nor did I panic. I was always aware of this possibility and had war-gamed it with my team. This meant that we were not surprised (I'll admit I was upset, scared and pissed off, but not surprised), and the contingency plans had already been developed. Security, I found, was preparing for the best, the worst and everything in between, but always hoping for the best. Living in Cremorne puts us in close proximity to a beautiful Sydney beach called Balmoral, leading up to my last operation Michelle and I would go there several times a week to swim, walk and climb across the rocks. We spent this time talking about all the things that could happen as a result of the upcoming surgery; what happens if I died? What happens if I lost the use of my legs? What happens if...? These were not easy discussions, especially in the first year of marriage, but it provided us both with the security of knowing what could occur, and what we would each plan to do in that circumstance. Balmoral was a secure place to talk about these things. We always found it easier to discuss heavy topics when around water.

## 4. Concentration of Force

If there are multiple targets to attack, we are taught to concentrate on one or two at a time (depending on how large our force is in comparison), and then move on to the next. If we are defending, we are taught that it's best not to spread our forces too thinly. This is how the military concentrates force. It is even simpler when I applied this to the cancer fight. There is a shit-load of things going on in your head when there is a disease running around your body. Not only was I managing the current treatment of chemotherapy and all the side effects that this brings, but I had the prospect of ongoing treatment for an indefinite amount of months, followed by mop-up surgery. Then there was the question of whether or not the Army would still employ what was left of me at the end of this ordeal. At one stage in Darwin, I was confronted with the fact

I had just had a nut taken away from me and having an orgasm with no ejaculation. I had to choose between the ability to have children, or begin the treatment for a disease that was already life-threateningly overdue. I was still not sleeping more than two hours a night due to the pain from the tumour in my pelvis and most of my mates were either deploying on operations or undergoing Special Forces selection while I was sitting around unable to run 50 metres. My best mate's brother had just passed away in a tragic accident at a time when I could offer no support to him. After five years in the Army I was now living with my mum again and I had the distinct feeling that I was 10 years old with the mumps. To top all this off, I had a sort-of-ex-girlfriend down south who wanted to come up to Darwin and visit me after I had used the cancer excuse to get away from initiating a messy break-up. My mental capacity is limited at the best of times and, had I attempted to deal with all these issues at once, I would have most likely lost the hair on my head quicker than the chemo was doing it. Concentration of force to me was dealing with one thing at a time, maybe two, and putting the rest to the back of my mind until their turn came up. Essentially, this principle is one of prioritising your issues. The tricky part about issues is that if you do not properly deal with them they don't go away. I quickly learned to "bravely change the things I could, have the serenity to accept the things I could not, and develop the wisdom to know the difference" (this is modified from a quote I saw once and love it). Concentration of force is not about avoiding issues or deflecting emotions. It is using your mental, physical and spiritual strength to solve a number of high-end issues in a prioritised order and not spreading yourself too thinly.

## 5. Economy of Effort

This principle works in line with concentration of force, and it relates to doing as much as possible while expending as little energy as possible in the process. Effectively, economy of effort is all about not wasting valuable energy where it is not needed. Effort, like ammunition, and a positive attitude, is a finite resource. While I was conscious that I was prioritising all my issues and was effective in only dealing with one or two at a time, I also needed to ensure that I only spent as much energy as was needed to overcome a particular problem before moving on. Another term for economy of effort is being smart-lazy. In business and in everyday life, we often see people working harder than they really need to on a particular task. Usually it is the result of poor management, being too close to the job at hand or believing that unless we are working hard, we are not achieving anything. Fighting cancer is no different. If you are blessed enough to know an Australian soldier you will find that they generally "have the brains of a bear, the energy of a sea-turtle and the slyness of a fox". Soldiers are lazy when they can be, because they know that when it comes time to work, they will work bloody hard. This is the economy of effort – working hard when it is needed and then resting and relaxing as soon as you can. This is obviously a principle driven very much by personality. There are a lot of people who simply cannot relax and always need to be doing something. My close friend Sully has served for almost 30 years as an infantryman and is the epitome of the Australian soldier. I have worked with him as a friend as well as his officer and openly say that he is most dangerous, and most likely to get in trouble, when he is bored. He always needs to be doing something but that does not mean his mind is always active (far from it mate…). He can keep his hands and body doing menial tasks while allowing his mind to switch off. Keeping active is good but letting the mind switch off, power down or meditate is economy of effort and ensures that when things do get hectic, there is enough fuel in the tank to get the job done, again and again and again.

## 6. Offensive Action

If this book has not portrayed it, I am an aggressive person. Not in personality (as I like to think of myself as quite calm and mellow), but in my attitude towards solving problems. The biggest issue I have faced in life has been dealing with cancer, and I have fought it – aggressively. To me, the principle of offensive action has been the most critical and influential in my life to date. When I fought in the boxing ring, when I advanced across the battlefield with a troop of armoured vehicles, or when I walked into a hospital for another complicated operation, it was always with an offensive attitude. If you don't like the term Offensive Action, you could easily replace it with Initiative. Sometimes the best offence is defence, and I found this to be true when I was reacting to the advancement of my disease. I was forced to have chemo due to a rapidly spreading cancer, but I saw this as an offensive action against this foe, I would visualize those chemicals coursing through my veins and arteries – tearing through cancerous cells like depleted Uranium ammunition going through a soft armoured vehicle. Having a testicle removed was not such a big sacrifice, if it meant delivering a counter-blow at cancer. Offensive action is about creating forward momentum and taking the initiative.

While you are moving forward and doing something, you feel like you are taking control of a situation and creating new options, even if it feels like there are none. A good analogy of offensive action, is that of a boxer in the ring against a bigger, stronger opponent. The smaller boxer needs a good defence to take the hits that are going to be dealt to him by a sweating hairy monster, but this does not mean he should be anything but offensive in his actions. Probably the worst thing that can happen to this boxer is to allow him to get backed in to a corner from where he has nowhere to go. Instead our boxer needs to always keep moving, if not forward, sideways, opening up new angles and options for him to take advantage of. He will still get hit at times. He is in a boxing ring, of course he'll take some hits, but providing he maintains an offensive attitude, he can keep working his opponent until that golden opening presents itself and he has the room to move in and hurt the big brute.

I have always been careful not to get too carried away with an offensive attitude, and allowing this to develop too far into an emotionally aggressive attitude – anger. Going back to our boxing analogy, I generally found that the moment a fighter lost his head to anger, he would lose. Allowing emotionally charged anger to take over your head space stops you from thinking clearly and rationally about the issue (or the opponent). Cancer returned in me for a second round, initially I got angry, really angry, but this achieved nothing except making me feel tired once the adrenaline ran out. Adrenaline is a great source of strength, but if we remember the economy of effort principle – it is wasteful to use it on something that achieves nothing. I was able to turn anger into determination. That helped my resolve and preparation for

the upcoming operation, but still allowed me to keep my head
while boxing the brute.

## 7. Sustainment

Every few months the media reports on the government's
intentions in regards to Afghanistan, and in particular, trying
to get a commitment on the length of stay for our forces in
this conflict. The government's response is always the same,
and I believe it's a valid and appropriate response. "We have
to accept that we will be in Afghanistan for a long time into
the future." This non-commitment is not political ducking
and weaving as much as a diplomatic but truthful way of
saying, "We have no idea how long this will take". COIN
warfare, like cancer, is a protracted campaign which cannot
be given an end-date. One of the most unique qualities of
fighting a COIN war is trying to determine who is the enemy.
When Coalition Forces first advanced into Iraq they fought
a conventional Iraqi Army. After defeating this enemy and
occupying the state, attention turned to *Al-Qaeda*. The longer
Coalition Forces occupied Iraq however, the more enemies
they had to contend with. Each had varying motivations,
intentions and capabilities. Even factions and groups that
originally supported the Coalition turned against them and
became adversaries. The Taliban and insurgents we are
fighting in Afghanistan now are not the same as we originally
removed from government in 2002/3. Interestingly, when the
pathology results analysing the latest malignant tumour came
back, they showed that the form of cancer then developing
inside me was not the same testicular cancer germ cell that I
was originally diagnosed with. Instead it showed properties of

a form of cancer more related to bowel cancer. The cancer I may fight in the future will probably not be the same cancer I have fought before, but rather different forms of cancer most probably caused by the treatment used during the initial years of treatment; this is a classical COIN characteristic.

Although, not in the news as much, the British are still conducting COIN operations in Ireland against the IRA (or break away cells of the IRA), and have been for a very long time. A big hurdle in my comprehension of cancer was accepting the fact that I would not be able to set a date for a mission-success proclamation. When I first got diagnosed I still remember asking Doc Honey if I should be over the fight in about six months. I was after all young and fit and... well maybe not so healthy. I believe she gave me that half-nod only to avoid me having to deal with too much bad news in one day. If I had known that after seven years I would still be dealing with this disease, I would have needed to use her shoulder to cry on (I should have done that anyway – she was a great looking lady). Seven years is really nothing when I contemplate the fact that this disease will be with me in one form or another, for what I intend to be a very long and full life. Even those people fortunate enough to detect cancer early, and are able to remove the threat before it spreads are forever affected mentally by the seemingly brief encounter. There is no doubt that cancer fucks with your mind. This is mainly because it pops up from under the radar – hiding within you until it has accumulated enough strength to strike. It can be like trying to fight your own shadow except that usually your shadow doesn't have the ability to hit you back so hard.

This is why sustainment is such an important principle. Without it we will experience burn-out and that will lead to, among other things, depression – something we cannot afford to have during our war. I realised about four years into my fight that this thing was not going away. I remember that day clearly because I had just had an appointment with Dr Rather-be-Fishing, and it was after returning from China. I truly thought I had seen the end of this disease. The reason why I remember the day so well though is because I had only just made it back to my car when the realisation hit with full force and tears fell (again). I was horrified at the prospect of someone seeing a soldier in uniform crying.

Sustainment is concerned with not only understanding that this fight will take years, if not a lifetime, but also about setting a tempo that allows your forces to continue the fight indefinitely. The human body and spirit are both incredibly durable. They can endure more than they would like to let you think, even more if we are able to get the two systems working together. But they need to be paced, allowed recovery, and where possible, trained-up prior to each encounter. My medical team were doubtful as to whether my body would have been able to survive another massive operation, remembering that it was the seventh in as many years, each one getting progressively more invasive than the last. But I had been given six precious years of respite between operation six and seven, and I had used these years to my advantage in first resting and then rebuilding my body and spirit in case we had to go through another operation. The last operation was by far the most invasive, and most difficult to recover from, but I have. Seven months on from the operation and I am still exhausted from the ordeal and I know I have at least another operation to deal with sometime in the future (neither myself or Dr Chocolate-Love are in any great hurry), but I have a good tempo now, and I have time to lick my wounds before I start re-building, and it will be sustainment that will get me through future operations, and a lot of surfing.

## 8. Maintenance of Morale

Morale is the bread and butter of an effective fighting force. Good morale will turn lambs into lions, and bad morale will do the opposite. Morale is one of those X-factors or the wild-card that could be your strongest ally one day, and then, without careful maintenance, is aligned with your enemy the next. Like cancer, when morale is bad it tends to lodge itself inside you with a niggling fear or a degree of uncertainty. It will then creep and infest, subtley taking hold of your forces and rendering them useless. The great thing about morale though, is that it takes very little to lift and maintain, if you are vigilant.

Morale could be closely aligned with hope. But even if there is no hope as to the outcome of a situation, morale can still be kept high, and can generate hope when all seems lost. I always saw the value of high morale, and that meant ensuring I maintained it constantly, which is really quite easy when you know what to look for.

Morale can be generated by anyone, everyone. I made sure I always surrounded myself with optimistic people – the kind of people that always see the glass as half-full as opposed to half-empty. Unfortunately we cannot always get away from morale/emotional vampires, so with these people I either attempted to lift their spirits, or if they were determined to be a sour-puss, I would just block them out of my thoughts and presence. This may sound harsh, but these people can bring bad morale into the camp, and for some reason they don't usually have half the shit going on in their life as the person with real problems – like the prospect of losing life or limb.

Morale can be generated by anything, everything. The smallest inanimate object can be used to generate morale if you approach it in the right way. Within seven days of waking up from my induced coma after my last operation, I asked the doctors if I could go outside for some sun. It was a logistical feat with my wheelchair not only carrying me, but also drains, pumps and monitors. It required two ICU nurses to accompany me and my entourage of family members in case any alarms began to scream. It took 60 mins of organising and arranging for me to be outside for 15-20 mins in the sun, half of that time I spent nodding in and out of exhausted sleep, but God did it feel good! The weather is nothing short of sensational towards the end of March in Sydney. These little moments in the sun literally solar-charged my morale batteries and I held on to that warmth long after they carried me back into the ambient lighting of the ICU ward.

One night, I was going through a particularly painful and sleepless period. I was on self-administered morphine injections, but all that seemed to do was bring on dark hallucinations and very dry lips (I was obsessed with water and ice and had been since waking up). Night time was always the worst time for morale because all the family was gone. I knew I needed rest, and it was time to sleep but was unable to close my eyes (I was suffering from post-surgical insomnia). My mind wouldn't shut down or shut up and I was as uncomfortable as hell. What I did have next to me was a side table with a small kidney bowl and some sterilised water left by one of the nurses after using it to clean one of my drains.

With a shaky hand and a fair bit of effort I was able to reach out and pour the water into the bowl. I then simply dipped my fingers in the cold water, making little splashing sounds. This carried me off to the ocean, paddling into a three foot swell on my surfboard at Warriewood Beach (another one of my favourite breaks along the Northern Beaches). I have no idea how long I surfed the break that night, must have been hours, but it worked in taking me away from the place I was in, and my morale was so much better after that session in the waves.

Morale can lead to hope in hopeless situations. In this I mean that good morale can result from belittling the enormity of a situation and distracting people from the seriousness of a situation and it often comes in the form of humour. I have heaps of examples for this. Dr Bow-tie's bow tie for instance. Nobody wears a bow tie nowadays…except this man. It is refreshing and iconic and when he walks into the room, it lifts morale because everyone notices it and forgets about the situation that brought him into the room in the first place. My godson – Leo (Todd's boy), came and visited me one day when I was in the ICU and hooked into everything that beeped. His eyes were wide with intrigue and wonder at all that was coming in and out of me. We had him believing that this was a part of my space ship and I was busy flying around looking for aliens or something. The joy and wonder in his eyes made me feel pretty good about being "plugged in". Morale is just as infectious as an air-borne disease. Giving the doctors a strong look into their eyes, commenting on the weather every morning (even if I had no idea what it was like), and squeezing their hands with all the strength I could muster when I shook hands with them, surprised and impressed them and they commented on this as a good sign of my recovery.

This in turn impressed me and I caught back what I had given them. This little storm of morale kept circling every time someone new came to see me and was vital to my recovery.

## 9. Surprise

Without a bit of imagination, the concept of surprising a non-sentient disease inside you may be a bit hard to grasp. So put on your creative helmets and stay with me...

From a military point of view, surprise keeps your enemy on the back foot. If our aim is to create offensive action and gain forward momentum, that would mean denying the enemy his ability to take offensive action. When we achieve the element of surprise, we are unpredictable to our enemy. It may also include posturing our forces and positions in a way that would lead our enemy to think we are going to attack from the front, while in truth we are actually going to attack from the left, the right or the rear. The art of deception is the key to surprise.

It would seem that the element of surprise was always on the side of cancer in this fight. I never expected to be diagnosed with this disease and consequently every time I thought I had it beaten, it would do something unexpected. Cancer is the guru of ambushes – the surprise attack. It sits and waits inside causing damage even before we know it's there. Furthermore, when symptoms do start to emerge we tend to believe it's something else. Therefore the first factor to the surprise principle is to deny the disease its ability to surprise us. I only got the meaning of this principle a few years ago. Sherlock Holmes claimed, "It is not until you remove the impossible that everything becomes possible". If we accept all possibilities regarding our fight with cancer, then we deny it the ability to surprise us. It also allows us to formulate plans to combat any approach the disease takes or leads us to taking. This also removes a degree of fear that comes with any bad news. In the lead up to a number of my operations my specialists asked me the same question almost verbatim;

"Now Matthew, you are aware that there is the possibility that this operation could kill you?" (If only I had thousand dollars for every time I was asked that question...).

"What will happen Doc if I don't have the operation?" Would always be my counter-question.

"You'll die." There you have it Doc.

I don't like being in these situations, and they don't seem to get easier despite their repetitiveness, but it is important to know the bad outcomes as well as the good – so there are no surprises. A good shot of morale lets you swallow the bad news with more ease.

My imagination gets even more carried away when I think of surprise in a second way. I like the element of surprise. I love doing and saying things unexpectedly, and would like to think that I am not too predictable (like telling everyone that I would love to leave the Army and become a florist – which is something I would actually like to do, some day. I even have a name in mind but I have not yet patented it so I'm not telling). Harnessing the element of surprise was something I needed to have against cancer, so I gave it to myself. I mentioned very early in this book that it was not until I saw cancer as an enemy that I could engage in combat, that I began to feel more comfortable in my situation. I had already more or less personified my disease as something outside me that I could fight. The concept of surprising cancer is a total figment of my own imagination that…works. Every time I underwent some form of treatment or operation, I imagined that I was attacking the disease and in some way doing something it did not expect. This carries on into all my principles and attitudes towards cancer, but essentially, I am always thinking of different ways to surprise and knock my enemy off-balance. Instead of believing that a particular surgery is the final option left to me, I consider it a perfectly timed, well planned attack that goes in and hits the bastard where it hurts, and when he wasn't expecting it.

## 10. Flexibility

Have you ever noticed that during gale force winds some trees are ripped up from their roots, while others are able to remain standing? Often it is the larger tress with thick trunks that are the ones knocked over. It is a result of my interest in Tao-ism while in China, that has me quoting: "It is the supple tree that bends in the wind which will remain standing after the larger, stronger, resistant ones are downed". Warfare, especially when operating against a strong opponent is similar. It's a game of stress and pressure points where each side presses and pushes and prods, looking to find the weak point in the other's defences, all the time bending under the weight of attacks and not allowing a breach to occur in their own defence. The pressure of cancer is huge and heavy and backbreaking, if you let it. But you don't have to be particularly strong to handle this pressure, as long as you can bend a little and displace the weight.

The first lesson I learned in flexibility was right at the start with my stupid racist ideas. I could have stuck to my misconceptions and asked for a different oncologist, but that would have meant denying myself an extremely valuable asset, and also a good friend (Dr Not-Caucasian). I was fortunate enough to learn quickly that any concept I had up until that point was probably wrong where it came to generalising about people and races. My next lesson in flexibility was accepting that there may be something for me to gain from alternative medicines, meditation and the whole "angel-world" – a very un-Army concept. The fact that most of these methods did not work for me is not important. What is important is that I realised how little I understood about a great many things, and that knowledge allowed me to investigate and develop a true understand of new and amazing things. In fact, through this understanding I have learned that one of the best exercises I could do in fighting cancer, is yoga, mainly because it teaches me to bend my mind, as well as my back.

Lastly, flexibility is a good principle to have because it teaches a final lesson. Once we have learned and begun to apply these principles, we need to be prepared to change them if need be. Flexibility reminds me that something may not work forever, and I should be willing to change, to bend in the wind, if need be.

At my pinnacle of living the alternative lifestyle I remember saying to people; "I will never undergo chemotherapy again. I will never have an operation again. If I have to fight cancer, it will be through alternative medicines and organic foods!" Big call – and I meant it at the time. But as much as I lived that lifestyle and believed that I could cure cancer in that way – it didn't happen. This disease is a flexible one. It can change and adapt to treatments and develop new principles. In order to defeat it, we need to be more flexible, more adaptive. Mohammed Ali was one of the greatest boxers of his time, arguably of all time, not because he was bigger or stronger than all of his opponents (in fact as a heavy weight he was one of the smaller guys in his class), but because he was fast both with hands and feet, and with the ability to change his technique as soon as his opponent thought he had him worked out. His ability to achieve so many come-backs was because he adapted to each fighter he came up against. Taking a pounding always seemed to make him stronger.

Generally, I don't think people are flexible enough. We seem to have made up our mind about something before we know any of the details. We hate being wrong. We hate not being in control and we really don't like being told to do something we don't want to do. In the last seven years I have been proven wrong, repeatedly, lost complete control of everything (including my bowels), repeatedly and had to do things that I really didn't want to do, repeatedly. Ironically these ordeals have battered strength into me rather than out of me. I know how I would like to live the rest of my life from here on in, but I am wise enough now to know that things will happen outside of my control, and it'll be my ability to adapt to these changes as opposed to taking them head on, that will define my success.

# TRAINING FOR WAR

*"You have to be fighting fit, to be fit to fight…"*

The one weapon that has never failed me during my fight was my attitude to training. The desire to be as prepared as possible before each battle has, in my eyes, been the deciding factor in my success to date against cancer. And I am far from an elite athlete.

I would put money on the fact that most people, when they read the title of this principle, will automatically envisage boot camp, soldiers running through obstacle courses with bayonets fixed to rifles and smoke and explosions going off. So what images would go through your head if this principle was titled "Training for Cancer"? How could someone possibly train themselves in preparation for a disease?

Forget for a minute the physicality of training (especially if you are the type of person that does not really enjoy exercise), and consider what the essence of training actually is. In my view, training disciplines the mind to focus on an aim. Fitness, strength, coordination, good reflexes, improved skill and the desire to improve/succeed are all by-products of the process of training the mind to achieve an aim. For someone to succeed, in any sport, vocation or war they require training, so why would fighting cancer be any different? If you think you will survive cancer without putting in the effort to train for the fight, you will have as much chance as a one-armed librarian will have stepping into the boxing ring against Mike Tyson.

Training the body and training the mind go hand in hand. Rarely will you train one without inadvertently training the other. A fight with cancer is as mental as it is physical.

Physically, it is not as hard as you would think, even if you are going into the battle out of shape. Cancer wants to stop you dead in your tracks, so your goal in training is to keep moving. I learned that being able to bench press 140 kgs did absolutely nothing to improve my ability to wrestle cancer. It didn't give a shit how big or strong or fast I was. In fact, Dr Rather-be-Fishing directed me to lose weight before my operation – because it is harder for the surgeons to work around the bulk of a 30 year old front rower than it is to work on a slim 70 year old woman. However, the big difference between the two is that the 30 year old can usually recover quicker. What my physical training did was strengthen my heart. Muscles will grow and waste away, cardio-vascular fitness can be improved with time and patience, but the heart is the organ which must keep pumping through the operations, chemotherapy and infections. Any activity that you can do which gets you moving and your heart pumping will be effective, so don't let the sickness from chemo or depression stop you from doing something – keep moving!

When I take the time to notice how I am feeling during exercise, I can feel every principle I have spoken about improving and sharpening, especially morale because it proves to me I still have some kick left in me. When I have advised people on personal training my first question is – "What activity do you like doing?" because that will always be the foundation of the training they should do. Your training must feel good as well as do good, because it is this motivation for activity and movement which will soon be used to directly combat cancer. Before I was diagnosed – when I was "healthy" – I had a very limited idea of training. Weights, fighting arts, rugby, combat training and drinking (to round off my social training) was all I knew. Yoga was for poofs, surfing was for pot-heads and walking was for old people. Now anything goes, anything I am able to do which gets me moving is great. Training and setting short-term goals is also a great way of monitoring recovery and progression after a big fight, more so in the mid to late stages of recovery when improvement is harder to detect. After every one of my last four operations it always started with the struggle to walk from bed to the toilet. Then the bench mark would be to walk 10, 20, 30 metres without stopping. After these initial steps I would look to achieve another lap in the pool, 10 minutess on the rowing machine or a walk up a steep hill. Cancer is going to have to do better than that if it is going to have a chance at slowing me down. I've got plenty of time to get fitter.

Mentally, you can train even when it is impossible to move. An active mind will drive an inactive body. Imagining that I would be paddle boarding in six months from my last operation, was as essential as my first step out of the wheelchair. Being able to paddle board indicates the probability that I will be surfing by Christmas time (I made this goal with two months to spare). Likewise, if all I could do from now on is walk the dog, then that is still a win.

I have mentioned previously the dangers of depression when fighting cancer. Depression can paralyse the mind and grind everything to a halt. Mental training needs to occur in order to keep your mind, and motivations moving forward. The doctors can fight your cancer without you being awake, but no-one can fight your depression but you, and the best way to fight it is by not letting it in your head in the first place. When a soldier is killed within a unit, and the troops return to their base, there exists a real danger of fear and depression infiltrating into the unit. Morale can drop and everyone ponders their own mortality or the worthiness of the fight they are in. A successful leader will get the men moving, get them training or out on patrol again. Inactivity is dangerous in a war zone, and the sooner the troops have purpose the safer everyone is and the more resilient they become. Driving yourself and your team through this dark point can only be achieved with discipline and focus. Discipline and focus can only be achieved through training.

# THE LEADER ON THE BATTLEFIELD, FEAR VERSUS COURAGE AND A GOOD DOSE OF HUMOUR

An effective leader is a good manager, a good commander and an excellent motivator. A leader doesn't exist without a team to lead. And a leader must always accept the consequences for a decision made. In my war with cancer I have two primary jobs; 1) To fight, and 2) To lead my team (by example and resolve). If you are fighting cancer, you are the only constant, besides the disease, on the battle field. Everyone else will come and go and no matter how much you are surrounded by loved ones, there will always be times when you feel completely alone.

Regardless of what the cancer is, or the treatment undergone, my first responsibility to myself, and everyone on my team, is to fight. People watching a fight with cancer from the side are either dealing with previous memories of the disease, or fearing that one day, they too might have to go through a similar ordeal. Fighting this disease tooth and nail, not only gave me hope, but I think also gave hope to everyone around me, and that made me feel special and worthy of the task.

On the battlefield a leader is surrounded by troops; hard fighting, cunning and intelligent, strong and ferocious, each of them with strengths and weaknesses, and ready to plough into the enemy – all of them in need of your direction. This war with cancer you find yourself in is yours to fight at the front line and that means taking responsibility for the planning and execution of operations. At the beginning of my journey I always responded to the doctor's suggestions with; "Do what you have do Doc, I'll be right". In retrospect I was happy for the doctor to do whatever he liked, without me taking responsibility for the outcome. I didn't see that I had a choice. Now I like to know all my choices, explore the avenues of approach, and if a treatment is to be decided upon, it is mine to decide on. I needed to take ownership of the decisions and accept the consequences of these actions were.

Fear has been a constant companion. It is ever present in varying degrees, and I would be lying if I said that I have not been scared shitless of when my journey may end and how I may meet it. This is, I think, a pretty natural emotion, and I think I would be more worried if I didn't feel this fear. Individually fear will effect us all in different ways. Some may charge towards the source of the fear in an attempt to eliminate it, while others may turn and flee or be paralysed into doing nothing. In the face of fear I have charged head-on towards it, but that doesn't mean I wouldn't have loved to have run away, I just don't see that I have a choice.

Fear is mostly generated by the unknown. Combating fear entails good training, preparation and a good understanding of all the different possible outcomes. There is nothing wrong with being scared of cancer, because it hurts, and because it can lead to something we have absolutely no idea of – death. Just because you are scared, does not mean you cannot be courageous. Courage is not the absence of fear, but the ability to continue to function, and achieve your aim, in the presence of fear. If my story has taught me one thing, it is that I believe myself now to be courageous.

"I am a soldier, not an author, why would I write a book?" Because if in writing this book I am able to help one other person to find the courage they need to fight their disease, then my battle-scars have not been earned in vain…

One last comment concerning having a sense of humour – get one, keep it, you're going to need it.

# ACQUIESCENCE

The air has a crispness to it that whispers of the encroaching winter, the sun however, already well above the watery horizon, still burns with an intensity that protests the end of summer. It is one of those perfect autumn mornings in Sydney. The Northern Beaches are already surging with activity as weekenders make the most of the hot, sun-drenched days as they are obviously on the retreat.

I survey the battlefield before me like a Field Marshall. Sets of waves rise gracefully, silently up from an expansive ocean as if they were ranks of aquatic soldiers advancing upon the ragged defences of terra firma. They rise higher and higher, lurching above the rocky outcrop with the intent to overwhelm and consume. From somewhere under the water the coastline's defences suddenly bite into the advancing wave's momentum, as though it had been waiting in ambush for the perfect moment to reveal its strength. There is a violent explosion of water and foam and spray. Some of the wave continues to advance, now meagrely, up over the rocks, its strength all but spent. The majority of water withdraws back and is reconstituted at the fore of the next wave, reinvigorated. With more intensity this wave throws itself at the staunch rock citadel, but with the same result. The offensive continues for another two waves and then all appears calm, except for the ominous ripple some 500 metres further out to sea that indicates Neptune's intent to continue the charge. It is a wondrous sight, it is the meeting of an unstoppable force with an immovable object and somewhat upsetting that I am looking at it through the eyes of a soldier that translates most things into an analogy of war.

On one side of me stands Pete, his warm and friendly eyes betray the excitement welling inside of him at the thought of going out into the middle of that eternal struggle and harness its energy by riding a 10 foot fiberglass plank. His experience in the surf is borne from hundreds of hours of conditioning and harsh lessons. On my other side is Kieran. Shorter in stature but big on personality. Whereas Pete is tall and lean, the K-train is shorter, nimble and holds the coiled energy of a ten year-old, always waiting to be released. K-train and I have surfed with each other for years. We originally met when I joined the Army and made friends with his brother Dave, and one Christmas was invited out to meet the rest of the family – fourteen of them in total, including mum and dad. At that meeting Kieran was 14 years old. I remember beating the shit out of him and his other young brothers in the family dining room because they were being smart-arses and thought they could take me on. Following that testosterone-induced introduction, K-train had joined the Army (like five of his brothers), and was posted to Sydney as a draughtsman. I had become an officer, been diagnosed with cancer and thought it timely to learn how to surf. Four years ago he and I were re-acquainted and had conducted raids along the beaches of NSW in search of waves ever since. Being the worst of the surfers in our trio, I looked upon this morning's challenge with trepidation.

"Woohoo, some of those sets are around five or six feet. Look at that right-hander, Matty!" K-train was physically leaning forward in his excitement.

"Yeah we should get some good rides out of those babies." Pete was more mellow in his comments, but he was already walking back to his truck to get his board and there was a spring in his step.

We had met Pete through this new sport that I had talked K-train into trying with me – Stand Up Paddle Boarding, or SUPing. My last operation had required the surgical team to saw through my sternum and when they had closed me back up the doctors had used wire to keep the chest plate together. That wire won't ever be leaving me and that means I can feel it rub through my skin every time I lay on a surfboard. It isn't the greatest feeling, and is similar to scraping your fingernails down a chalkboard. It doesn't really hurt, but it is definitely uncomfortable. As the name implies, SUPing involves standing on a board right from the get-go. It is a cross between surfing and canoeing and a long paddle is used to propel you through the water. On flat water this activity is relatively easy and an excellent rehabilitation tool. In the surf, it can be very challenging, but extremely fun. Since being diagnosed with testicular cancer seven years earlier, I have made it a priority to remain as fit and healthy as possible and also try absolutely anything I can physically attempt. Through that journey I had discovered surfing and now SUPing. Pete is a genius on the SUP, K-train has picked it up effortlessly. I am a different story, but the one thing I have on my side is dogged determination.

We finally slide out onto the water and begin our advance towards the conflict zone. The other two steam ahead of me, long powerful strokes that are paced by deep rhythmic breaths. My lungs hold me back a little. Several months of chemotherapy, two lung operations and an arterial graft has left me somewhat breathless, I need to ease into activity at a slower rate to accommodate the oxygen recovery and allow my heart to catch up.

Pete is the first out behind the break and immediately stamps his back foot to the rear of the board, making a wide circular paddle stroke that pivots his massive board 180 degrees. He remains in this stance but his strokes become more linear, driving the SUP forward in the same direction as a mountain of water that is looming up behind him. As the wave reaches his board, it picks him up and accelerates him until he is racing down the face of a wall of water, turning and carving up water as though he were the blade of a knife. Kieran is the next to hitchhike on one of these watery steam trains, and I see him squealing with delight as he is flung down the face of five foot of wave. We continue to play in this wonderland for a while and I have been slowly edging towards the take-off point of the larger waves.

In my earlier years, during tactical training, I would often rush toward an enemy's defensive position without due consideration to flank or rear security and would be punished for doing so by red faced instructors. As a boxer, I was happy to expose an opening to my opponent in an attempt to draw him in, wearing some hits in the process, but getting him in the right position to dominate the fight. Even when I was first diagnosed with cancer, and the doctor was explaining the magnitude of my initial abdominal operation, that among other things was possibly going to leave me a quadriplegic, or dead, I had looked at it as a challenge, something to wrestle and dominate. But along the way, in amongst seven or so operations, blood pressure complications, nerve damage and circulatory issues, I seem to have lost a bit of that aggression and in its place is a quieter determination that gave cautious respect to the challenges I faced.

Right now though, I find myself nervously observing a shape in the distance which is rising upwards as quickly as it is racing towards me. The other two are further towards the beach, either riding a wave or returning from one. It's just me out here, alone and facing a demon that sees me as very insignificant. Now that I'm here I am wondering if it was such a great idea to come out today, five foot my arse, this thing looks huge! Like my fight with cancer, it doesn't really matter anymore how I got here, I am now in a position where I am going to have to deal with the challenge and…paddle like hell.

I shift towards the back of the board and make a turn with none of the ease that Pete is able to. But at least I am still upright and facing the proper direction. A nervous glance over my shoulder proves that the wave is threatening to block out the sun and white foam at its tip looks suspiciously like snarling fangs. Cold resolve takes command of me now and I hunch down and start paddling hard in an attempt to gain enough speed to survive the take-off, at the same time lowering my centre of gravity for better balance. I can feel myself being picked up. At 100 kgs I feel like an umbrella caught by a gale force wind and I am lifted from what I thought would be sea-level up one, two, three feet and climbing. Four, five, six feet and I suddenly have a great perspective of life. Pete and K-train are small dots down below and the beach and coastline stretch out further than I had notice before. I am floating somewhere in between the cold wet reality of earth and the untouchable clouds above. And then the drop begins. I know I shouldn't look down, I should be looking towards where I want to be going, but the abyss below is frighteningly alluring to resist. I am going fast now, at a pace where adrenaline overrides caution and I drag my gaze up to the face of this bomb willing my body to follow. I dig my paddle into the wedge of water and start heaving 12 foot of board to change direction. I can feel scar tissue along my abdominals starting to strain under the pressure, have they had enough time to heal since the last cut? Pressure on the rail of my board starts to unbalance me. I feel it and try to correct it by shifting the weight onto my right leg. It moves sluggishly, as the majority of the blood clot that formed 16 months earlier announcing the return of the cancer, still clings to my femur artery and it's permanently swollen out of proportion with that of the left leg. A sluggish move isn't acceptable in this situation and I can almost hear the roar of triumph as the monster I rode throws me from its face.

I have a split second that actually seems to last for an eternity. It is that moment when time seems to slow down even though you know it is moving quickly. Senses are heightened and your perspective is clear. I've known this moment before. It was the moment before I got tackled from the side in a rugby game, the time when the car I was driving in was pushed off the road at 120 kms/hour, the realisation that my guard was down and I was about to get a left hook to the jaw. It is the same moment I have felt every time I have gone back into hospital for another operation, and is my last real thought before the tingling heat of the anaesthetic consumes my consciousness. A single moment allows for a single action and my action is to take a breath.

Slam! I hit the water with a force that threatens to take away the breath I had just stolen. I am pretty sure I am contorted in a way that isn't natural as my right foot seems to be where my left should have been, and I seem to be forever tumbled and scrunched into tighter knots. Something hard bites into my left kidney, or where my left kidney used to be, had it not been lost some years ago during one of the operations. I guess that it's my board and it would have hurt more had the kidney been there. My primary concern remains on concentrating not to let go of the air in my lungs.

I am not panicking, not yet, I let this storm wash over me as I am used to not wasting energy at this time. I can feel my heart racing though, it is still weak and it is working hard under the strain I have just put it under and so when I feel the grip of the wave's fury relax a little, I strike out and make for the surface. There is a cord attached to my leg with the dead weight of my board indicating which way to go. I breach and gasp for air. It is a breath which I cannot saver for too long as I know that I am not out of danger yet. I still need to survive the next wave. I am not in a hospital bed fighting for breath, not this time, I am in the middle of the ocean and I am looking at another six foot wall of water falling on top of me. I dive back under the sheets and brace. I am actually having a morbid sense of fun. My lungs burn for air and my heart begins to falter, I can see stars exploding behind my eyelids. I need to hold on just a little while longer. The wave picks up my board and drags me along with it, up to the surface and I know that I have my window. I suck in an enormously insufficient breath of air and clamber up onto the board, riding the white wash of a third wave towards the shore. I barely have the energy to lie on the board.

As I sit on the beach at tide level I look out into the ocean and wait for my heart to relax and the stars to subside. That was pretty hectic − so was the last seven years − and I always seem to take this time to reflect on what I have gone through. Why do I keep putting myself in these situations? After all that I have been through should I not take it easy and take up lawn bowls? Because that's not my nature. At heart I am a soldier, a fighter. If my life is a burning candle than my flame will burn very bright. There is always a challenge out there to be faced.